Code 1

D0777997

JOURNEY
in the
RISEN CHRIST

JOURNEY
in the
RISEN CHRIST

The "Little Mandate" of
Catherine de Hueck Doherty

Rev. Robert Wild

ALBA · HOUSE   NEW · YORK

SOCIETY OF ST. PAUL, 2187 VICTORY BLVD., STATEN ISLAND, NEW YORK 10314

Library of Congress Cataloging-in-Publication Data

Wild, Robert A., 1936 —
        Journey in the Risen Christ : the "little mandate" of Jesus to
    Catherine de Hueck Doherty / by Robert Wild.
            p.   cm.
        Continues: Love, Love, Love. c1989.
        Includes bibliographical references.
        ISBN 0-8189-0635-9
        1. Doherty, Catherine de Hueck, 1896-1985.   2. Spirituality —
    Catholic Church — History of doctrines — 20th century.   3. Catholic
    Church — Doctrines — History — 20th century.   I. Title.
        BX4705.D56W559   1992   91-40305
        248.4'82 — dc20   CIP

Designed, printed and bound in the United States of
America by the Fathers and Brothers of the
Society of St. Paul, 2187 Victory Boulevard,
Staten Island, New York 10314, as part of their
communications apostolate.

PRINTING INFORMATION:

Current Printing - first digit   1   2   3   4   5   6   7   8   9   10   11   12

Year of Current Printing - first year shown
  1992   1993   1994   1995   1996   1997   1998   1999

CONTENTS

That's what Christianity is all about — the crucified Christ and the dancing Christ. The cross is but the pathway to the resurrection. (SLFF, October 7, 1973)

Resting in the arms of God . . . we must walk in the heat of the day . . . go through everything he did. But we know something that nobody else knew in his day. We know that we live in his resurrection. (COM)

INTRODUCTION

The Little Mandate

Arise — Go! Sell all you possess . . . give it directly, personally to the poor. Take up My cross (their cross) and follow Me — going to the poor — being poor — being one with them — one with Me.

Little — be always little . . . simple — poor — childlike.

Preach the Gospel WITH YOUR LIFE — WITHOUT COM-PROMISE — listen to the Spirit — He will lead you.

Do little things exceedingly well for love of Me.

Love — love — love, never counting the cost.

Go into the marketplace and stay with Me . . . pray . . . fast . . . pray always . . . fast.

Be hidden — be a light to your neighbor's feet. Go without fears into the depth of men's hearts . . . I shall be with you.

Pray always. I WILL BE YOUR REST.

This is my third and final volume presenting the above Little Mandate of the Lord to Catherine de Hueck Doherty. The first two volumes were: *Journey To the Lonely Christ* (1987), and *Love, Love, Love* (1989), also by Alba House. Catherine believed that these words expressed her vocation, her "Little Mandate from God."

In the previous volumes I gave short sketches of Catherine's life, in case the reader was not familiar with her. In this present work I will presume such familiarity. But even if the reader is not too acquainted with Catherine, this book will still be understandable. Perhaps it will whet the reader's appetite for my first two volumes as well as other books concerning Catherine's life and works. (See the bibliography for references.)

I call attention especially to her autobiography, *Fragments of My Life*, and to Emile Briere's *Katia*. Fr. Briere was perhaps Catherine's closest associate and confidant during the last twenty years of her life. His personal reflections are an important source for understanding this prophetic woman of our time. For those who have not read my two previous volumes, a brief description of the Lord's Mandate to Catherine, exclusive of the last three lines — the subject of the present book — may be helpful here.

SUMMARY OF THE LITTLE MANDATE

Catherine was born in Russia on August 15, 1896. When she was a young child of seven or eight she attended a convent school in Alexandria, Egypt, conducted by the Sisters of Sion. In the chapel of that school was a western crucifix — the first she had ever seen? — depicting blood flowing rather profusely from the Lord's wounds. One day she went into the chapel with soap and water and tried to wash the blood off! The inspiration behind this far from childish gesture grew into the great passion of her life.

What was that passion? To assuage the pain, the loneliness, the abandonment of Christ. She was given an extraordinary realization that, in the human race, Christ continues to suffer mystically.

"Christ is in agony until the end of the world. But Christ is in you and me. And what is more important, in the other fellow. What about them being in agony, my brothers and sisters? That, my friend, is what Madonna House is all about. Open your hearts; you have the key to do it. The Lord has given it to you in baptism. Open your hearts and let him in. Stop thinking about yourself and begin — honestly, truthfully, totally — thinking of others." (Family Letter, May, 1980)

In some real but mysterious sense, "the First and the Last," "the Living One," "the One who was dead and is alive forever," "the One who holds the keys of death and of Hades" (Rv 1:18) — in some way — this resurrected and glorious Christ is still suffering in his members (Ac 9:5). This theme is also central to the spirituality of other contemporary figures.

Fr. Werenfried van Straaten, a Dutch Norbertine (and one of the great men of our time), is the founder of an international organization called "Aid To the Church In Need." Over the past forty years he has begged and given away more than 600 million dollars. He is driven by the same passion which drove Catherine; he describes it beautifully:

> The essential part of my vocation is this: that whenever God weeps, I have to dry his tears. God, of course, does not weep in heaven, where he dwells in inaccessible light and eternally enjoys his endless happiness. God weeps on earth. Ceaselessly, his tears flow over the divine countenance of Jesus, who is One with the Heavenly Father and yet on earth lives on in the least of his people, and suffers, and starves, and is persecuted. The tears of the poor are his tears, because he has become one with them. And Jesus' tears are the tears of God. Thus God weeps in all the sad,

suffering, and sighing people of our times. We cannot
love him if we do not dry their tears. (*Where God Weeps*,
pp. xiv-xv).

In a recent book, *For the Least of My Brothers*, Omer
Tanghe, a priest associate of Madonna House, compares the
spiritualities of Catherine and Mother Teresa of Calcutta.
Mother Teresa understands Christ's "I thirst" from the cross
as referring to the continuation of his suffering in
humanity.

This theme is part of our western tradition. In the
words of Pope St. Leo the Great (5th Century): "The Lord's
passion is not over and done with; it will continue *until the
end of the world*. Just as in the saints it is Jesus who is honored,
in the poor it is Jesus who is fed and clothed, so in all who
suffer for doing right it is Jesus who suffers" (Sermon LXX,
On the Passion). And St. Caesarius of Arles, Sermon 25: "In
this life God feels cold and hunger in all who are stricken
with poverty; for remember, he once said: What you have
done to the least of my brothers, you have done to me.'
When the poor are starving, Christ too hungers. Christ
hungers now, my brethren; it is he who deigns to hunger
and thirst in the persons of the poor."

Catherine, then, was on a long journey to meet Christ in
every human person, to comfort and console him there, to
"wash the blood" from his wounds. The first paragraph of
the Mandate contains this central theme. She must "arise
and go" to attend to the lonely and forgotten Christ. The
journey requires a stripping of all things — "Sell all you
possess" — so she can embrace the cross of the poor which is
the cross of Christ. In this way she will attain union with
Christ — "one with Me" — since whatever we do to one
another we do to him.

The second line of the Mandate describes the various dimensions of the poverty necessary to reach Christ in the poor. One must be "little," realizing that everything is from God. This will bring us into a fundamental simplicity and transparency, a deeper spiritual poverty through which God can work most effectively. Above all, it will make us childlike, restoring us to our basic inheritance as children of the Father. As children of God, we become channels of his grace, and help to restore the image of God in others.

These first two lines were the topic of my first volume.

In the second volume I treated lines three, four and five. When we are as transparent as children, the Gospel, which is the presence of the risen Christ within us, will be preached, that is, made present in every aspect of our lives. But it must be made present "without compromise," that is, *passionately*, intensely. To be in love with God is to be *uncompromisingly in love.*

The Holy Spirit, if we truly listen to him, will bring to our minds all the Lord has said to us, and will show us how to love. Especially will he help us perform the ordinary tasks of everyday life with great love. In this way, wherever and however people encounter us, they will also meet the Risen Christ *whom we bear within.*

You might say that lines two to five express more our *preparation* for the journey; lines six, seven and eight — the subject of this present book — point to our destination, where we are going.

And where are we going? We are going into the market-place, into the depths of men's' hearts, to be a light for their feet on their journey. Prayer — "Pray always" — is both food for this journey and, amazingly, the final goal — "I will be your rest."

The last line is the promise that, if we keep trying to center our whole lives on God through prayer and love, the

Lord himself will become our rest. This "rest" means several things, but mostly it refers to an ever greater faith awareness that *we are already living in the risen Christ*. That our whole journey takes place *in the risen Christ* is the central theme of this last volume.

JOURNEY IN THE RISEN CHRIST: HUPHSOS

The lonely Christ. The risen Christ. We are confronted with a paradox: in a most mysterious way the risen Christ has a Body that can still suffer, and which still does suffer, as we can all testify. It was the risen Lord who met Paul on the road to Damascus, and who said to him, "Why are you persecuting Me?" Christ's joy and pain are joined in a single Body.

As Catherine pilgrimages to console the lonely Christ she experienced this strange duality of suffering and joy. Every act of love was simultaneously a com-passion in the suffering of Christ and a new experience of his resurrected joy. The *journey to the lonely Christ* is at one and the same time a *journey in the risen Christ*.

St. Cyril of Jerusalem, speaking about the descent of the candidates into the baptismal pool, described it as both a dying and a rising. And this is true of every act of selfless love. As a self-emptying, it is pain. And precisely because of the death to selfishness, one should be better able to experience the new life within — the joy of the risen Christ. In fact, Catherine insisted that the only reason we empty ourselves is to be filled with Christ. As we shall see, the "rest" of the last line refers primarily to an ever greater awareness and realization of living in the risen Lord.

As a result of modern biblical studies some new words

have entered our popular Christian vocabulary. From the Hebrew we have learned "anawim," which means the poor and faithful remnant awaiting the Messiah. From the Greek of the New Testament we picked up the word "diaspora," "scattering," referring to the Christian communities scattered abroad like seed in the world; and "parousia," "appearance," referring to the second coming of the Lord.

Another new word expressing an aspect of the Christian life very dear to Catherine's Russian soul is "kenosis," "emptying," referring to the self-abasement of the Word Incarnate: "Have this mind in you that was in Christ Jesus who, being in the very nature God . . . made himself nothing" (literally, "emptied himself," *ekenosen*; Ph 2:5-7). "Kenosis" expresses the cross dimension of our pilgrimage — the journey to the lonely Christ and into the pain of the world. But two lines later in Philippians is the "other side" of that life: "Therefore God *exalted him* to the highest place."

I don't know how new words like anawim, diaspora, and kenosis enter our vocabulary. I suppose enough scholars would have to write about it, and then the word is used in books and catechesis. I'm sure my little book will not be enough to effect this, but I wish somehow another new word would enter our vocabulary. I ardently suggest the word "*huphsos.*" It is the Greek word for "height" or "heaven," but especially, by metonymy, means a spiritual height. It is the technical word used for the Lord's own "uplifting."

In St. John we read: "As Moses lifted up the serpent in the desert, so must the Son of Man be lifted up . . ."(3,14); "when you have lifted up the Son of Man, then you will know that I am He" (8,28); "and when I am lifted up from the earth, I shall draw all people to myself" (12:32). In all these texts the same verb is used — *huphsoo* — "to be lifted up, to exalt."

Commentators point out that when Jesus set his face

towards Jerusalem he began his ascent, his *huphsos*, his final "uplifting" in the three-fold movement of being lifted up on the cross, being raised from the dead, and being exalted to the Father's right hand. *"Huphsos,"* therefore, means more than the resurrection: it is Christ's whole exaltation to glory by the Father precisely because he was obedient to the Father's will and humbled — emptied — himself.

The Christian life essentially consists in living, even now, in the fulfillment of Christ's prayer before he died: "I want those you have given me to be with me where I am, so that they may see the glory you have given me" (Jn 17:24). What has happened to Christ, has happened to us. This was the belief and awareness of the early Christians: "And God raised us up with Christ and seated us with him in the heavenly realms" (Ep 2:6). "Since, then, you have been raised with Christ, set your hearts on things above, where Christ is seated . . ." (Col 3:1).

Consequently, those who are joined to Christ through his Spirit have also "been exalted" with him. Although we have not yet passed through physical death, in our deepest reality we are already on the other side of death. Every true act of love, every act of dying to our old self(ishness), should enable us to realize more and more the truth of our being: we are already raised and exalted with Christ.

Like Lazarus, we are already out of the tomb, standing in the sunlight. The Lord said, "Unbind him." Every act of love arising from faith should help to remove the bandages from our spiritual eyes. When bandages are removed there is a brief pain, a tearing, which may momentarily obscure our vision of the light. As in physical darkness, so in the darkness of pain, it takes a little while to readjust our eyes. The cross is the removal of the bandages. We should never experience a death without a rising.

Catherine's book *Strannik* (Pilgrim) is very important

for understanding her vision of the Christian life. *"Strannik"* is her symbolic Russian word expressing the final stage of the journey — the stage of integration.

The pilgrim is one who has internalized the dimensions of community and poustinia — the journey into the hearts of others and into the Heart of God — and is now simply available to the Wind of the Spirit, poised for the Father's will. And the pilgrim has arrived precisely at the realization of the resurrection: "Now the pilgrim begins in the fullness of the resurrected Christ. He has followed Christ through his Incarnation and his passion; and he was ready to be crucified. That's when he realized that Christ is with us, and the miracle of his presence is the eternal miracle of the resurrection. He [the pilgrim] now functions, lives, has his being, breathes the resurrection" (St 69). Since baptism our whole being has been immersed in the resurrected Christ. On each step of our journey, whether joyful or painful, we should become more aware of this new life within us.

WITHOUT FEAR INTO HEARTS

The overall effect of sin, of our disorientation from God, is fear: "The Lord God called to the man, 'Where are you?' He answered, I heard you in the garden, and I was afraid because I was naked; so I hid.' " (Gn 3:9-10)

Our faith-vision of reality is personal. Catherine often taught us that "we have come from the mind of God and are returning to the heart of God." And we are destined by God to be united with one another: ". . . that they may be one as You and I are one." The Mandate maps the long journey from behind the trees of the garden to walking once again in the cool of the evening, in open friendship with God and with one another.

In the last three lines of the Mandate which we are about to consider, "pray" occurs three times. Prayer emphasizes the journey into the Heart of God — Father, Son and Holy Spirit. Although Mary is not mentioned explicitly in the Mandate, we are also on a journey into her heart. As Catherine used to say, "Christ is the way to the Father, but Mary is the Gate to Christ." I will treat of Mary under the title of Our Lady of Combermere.

The phrases of the Mandate, "marketplace," "neighbor's feet," and "men's hearts," refer primarily to the journey *into human hearts*. These words are symbols of the final integration of prayer and service of neighbor.

We all sense, in the depths of our being, a brokenness and fragmentation. In the garden before the fall there was no prayer *and* work, prayer *and* marketplace. Our whole being was immersed in the contemplative presence of God; and tending the garden did not distract us from that Presence. It is only after the fall that life was broken up into "work" and "prayer." The Mandate calls us to return to the wholeness of Eden. The Lord is already *in* the marketplace, already *in* men's hearts. But we are not completely united to the Lord.

Because of our lack of wholeness, prayer must be considered from various perspectives: as helping us enter the marketplace; as giving us strength to remain there; as resting in the Lord once we attain some measure of union. "Pray always" especially symbolizes the final integration. It means that whatever we are doing we should always be walking with the Father in the cool of the evening. Perhaps the final goal of the Mandate could be stated as always reposing on the breast of God while serving with passionate love in the marketplace.

A GOSPEL VERSION FOR THE WHOLE
OF LIFE

When Catherine came to North America in 1921 she experienced that the Gospel was absent from much of our culture. In the "New World" of North America we have never really experienced anything approaching a Christian culture such as existed in Russian before the revolution, or in the Western Europe in the centuries of faith.

Since the time of her pioneering racial justice in the 30's and 40's, North America has experienced more of a thrust of the Gospel into society. Still, sociologists and cultural analysts are telling us that, in the last quarter of this century, we are entering another age of public apathy. We are experiencing the "fall of public man," and the "naked public square" (titles of books documenting this withdrawal). The present "habit of the American heart" is pretty much to take care of oneself.

Catherine was fond of saying, "A stranger is a friend I haven't met yet." "Stranger" is an ominous word today. Children are now taught not to speak to strangers. This may be understandable and prudent in today's society, but it mirrors a new fear of one another, and a deterioration of public life. Catherine's spirituality has everything to do with preparing people to enter the marketplaces of human hearts and human activity.

But first of all, it is necessary to create environs — families, parishes, neighborhoods — with a Nazareth atmosphere where people can be nourished, nurtured, and formed in the love of God and neighbor. Then they will have the courage to venture forth into the marketplaces of the world, there to witness to the risen Christ.

Superbly attuned to the Lord's own life among us, Catherine insists that in this world the journey must end on

Golgotha. The Lord left Nazareth and walked the market-places of the world. But eventually he died in the market-place, totally naked and drained of every drop of blood for love of us. The journey to the lonely Christ in the risen Christ will lead us deeply into his heart and the hearts of all our brothers and sisters. But, in this world, it will mean crucifixion in the marketplace. Then, life everlasting!

It has been said that "the future belongs to the masses, so someone better tell them in very simple terms what reality is all about!" Catherine's Mandate is a simple — but far from easy — Gospel vision of how, by journeying in the risen Christ, we can be vehicles 9of his life and love to others. On a number of occasions people have said to me, "Thank God that Catherine spoke in simple language we lay people can understand!" I pray that I may be able to communicate her vision in the same way she did, that this book may be a simple and humble light to the feet of everyone on their way to everlasting life.

JOURNEY
in the
RISEN CHRIST

CHAPTER ONE

Go Into The Marketplace And Stay With Me

GO

Personal life is essentially movement towards, relationship with, the other. In the Trinitarian life
there is a perfect gift of Self — a movement towards the
Other — among the Three Persons. To save mankind the
Father asked the Son to *go* into the world; and after his
resurrection, Jesus commanded his disciples to likewise "go
into the world and proclaim the good news." At the heart of
life, then, is a constant call to *go forth.*

In the Mandate the word "Go" appears four times —
twice in the thematic first paragraph, and twice in the three
lines we are now considering. (And even in the second last
line where it is not stated explicitly, it is implied: "Go and be
a light to your neighbor's feet.") The Mandate directs our
steps in this life along our journey to the Father.

Very early in her apostolic life, Catherine was strug-
gling with the question of her vocation, where the Lord
wanted her to go. She came across the following poem which
expressed so well the depths of his answer that she included

it on the first page of the Constitution or "Way of Life" she wrote for her spiritual children in 1971:

> I said: Let me work in the fields. Christ said: No, work in the town. I said: There are no flowers there. He said: No flowers, but a crown. I said: But the sky is dark and there is nothing but noise and din. Christ wept as He answered back: There is more, there is sin. I said: I shall miss the light, and friends will miss me, they say. Christ answered: Choose tonight . . . if I shall miss you, or they.

She went into the town, into the marketplace.

INTO THE MARKETPLACE

What is the marketplace? In a geographic sense it is where the busy-ness of human, and especially public, activity takes place — the buying and selling, the joys and tragedies, the politics and expressions of culture. It is the streets and shops, the theaters and coliseums, the halls of parliament and council. "Marketplace" is the word we use in contrast to "desert" and "home" and being by ourselves.

But Catherine, in one of her commentaries on this line, first gives the word a more elemental meaning:

> What is the marketplace? Is it the secular city? Is that the actual marketplace? Is it the urban city, suburbia where all the supermarkets are? No. It's simply the *soul of man*. The marketplace is the soul of man, where man trades his soul either to God or to the devil, or to anyone in between . . . it is the supermarket of the spiritual world . . . the marketplace of souls. (COLM)

The activity of the public marketplace is simply a reflection of the marketplace which is the soul of man. It is in the human heart where all the trading, all the buying and selling, takes place. It is in the soul of man where deals are made, speeches given, revolutions planned, pacts made with God or the devil. "Go" is another word for "mission," and presently we will be discussing Catherine's concept of missionary activity. But it is precisely because the human heart is the primary marketplace that it is also the primary mission field:

> For we are, each one of us, an immense mission field which we must explore, cover, attend to, if we want to be of use to our brothers anywhere. How many of us refuse to do the real plowing, harvesting and seeding of our own 'mission field.' For some unaccountable reason I have dreamt that the Lord was sending me down into the mission field of each one of you. (SLFF #223, 1973)

"I SHALL VOMIT THE LUKEWARM OUT OF MY MOUTH"

Catherine leads us still deeper. When she comments on what happens in the marketplace, she often uses words like tepidity, indifference, and even vomit (Rv 7:16): "I shall vomit the lukewarm out of My mouth." When you get into the mire of this terrible tepidity, it is really like vomit all around you. That's the moment you want to turn away. That's the moment when all your spiritual, psychological, and physical powers say, "Lord, it is impossible." (Com)

The great sin against love is lukewarmness — which translated means *not caring*. We refuse the command to "go into the marketplace" when we don't care. We may be called to raise a family and be unable to be involved in public issues. It doesn't matter, as long as we care for our family. We may be called to a contemplative monastery and have no outside apostolate. It doesn't matter, as long as in prayer and community life we are directed outward and care for others. "Going into the marketplace" means caring, overcoming our fears of involvement:

> If you were given a mission to deal with, let us say, the Yukon, what would you think of a missionary who would hide himself within the cozy framework of his little or big mission house, if he seldom went out, if he established himself in sort of fortress-like walls that spell the words, "leave me alone, I am busy." Actually, these words spell, above all, fear of involvement with our brethren and with anyone who comes to us. (SLFF #23, 1958)

"Wisdom calls aloud in the streets, she raises her voice in the marketplace. She calls out at the street corners; she delivers her message at the city gates" (Pr 1:20-21). These Scriptures were literally and completely fulfilled when Divine Wisdom, Jesus, cried out in the marketplace in Jerusalem on the last day of the festival, "If any man is thirsty, let him come to me" (Jn 7:37-39).

So too, we are called to radiate the presence of Jesus in the marketplaces of the world for those who are dying of hunger and thirst; to minister to him in others; to make him known and loved. Whenever, either in ourselves or in others, we fail to care, we leave the Lord alone in his solitude. The prophetic call is to keep him company in the marketplaces of the world. "Choose tonight, whether I will miss you, or they."

WHAT DO WE DO IN THE
MARKETPLACE?
CATHERINE'S UNDERSTANDING OF MISSION

All countries are mission territories, that is, our own
heart and our own soul. And the mind and heart of every
neighbor. That's the country. The will of God for you, as
for all our missions, is contact with people. *It is unimportant
what form this contact takes.* (SLFF #23, 1958)

To me, this last sentence is truly astounding! What do
we do when we go into the marketplace? It's not important!
Our Mandate allows us the freedom to do anything. The
form our activity takes is not the essential thing. For
Catherine, the heart of missionary activity is *personal contact
with people.* "Interpersonal relationships in the Christian
sense means a loving contact, bringing the mystery of God's
presence in you to others." (*Ibid.*)

The Gospel is God's love for us manifested in Jesus. If
you meet people in a loving way, you are a missionary: "The
mystery of God's love in which he asks you to be present
where often his presence is not experienced. Yours is an
apostolate of bringing the Christ who dwells in you; and you
witness to him first of all by your presence."

Throughout her long life Catherine had been involved
in almost every form of the apostolate — lecturing to audi-
ences, teaching classes, feeding the hungry, clothing the
naked, finding lodging for the homeless, writing articles and
books. In all these activities her emphasis was always on *a
most personal contact with people.* If ever a particular apostolic
activity tended to become impersonal, she would rethink it.

Oftentimes, because of our fears, we unconsciously (or
consciously) seek impersonal ways of helping people. In our

modern world we have all experienced being helped by
people who don't even look at us.

Catherine's genius was always to concentrate on the
personal factor, so much so that "it is unimportant what
form this contact takes." She wanted people to be able to see
the presence of Christ in us. So whatever we may do, we
must be careful not to "help people" without this personal
touch. Nursing, teaching, handing out clothes, can become
impersonal, and thus fail to mediate the loving presence of
Christ.

Yes, people need clothes. Yes, people need advice. But
most of all they need to know God's personal love for them.
Everything we do must be a medium for this communication of the reality of God's loving presence.

When this loving contact takes place, all kinds of mira-
cles can happen. Relationships are established which no
amount of arranging and planning could ever have
achieved. Love opens peoples' hearts. And then we are able
to enter their hearts not just with clothes or food, but with
ourselves. Or rather, the presence of Christ whom we bear is
revealed to them. Even more deeply: The loving presence of
Christ within us gives birth to their awareness of Christ
within them.

IDENTIFICATION WITH THE OTHER

In Staff Letter 117, 1962, Catherine outlined her basic
approach to mission. She speaks specifically about our going
to foreign missions, in this case, Pakistan; but her teaching
can be applied to the whole Mandate:

> You can't presume that our western ideas and our white
> skin are passports to peoples' hearts. They're often a hand-

icap, a tremendous handicap to the giving of the glad news that God loved us first and calls us to a life of love with him. Our weapons are peace and charity. Love identifies itself with those it serves. We must not have the attitude of 'Lady Bountiful,' coming to these poor people to help them. We walk in humility, with a heart filled with gratitude that we have been permitted to serve our brothers and sisters in Christ in other parts of the world.

Catherine counsels us, first of all, to go to the poor humbly. It is a privilege to serve the poor. We should be grateful for the graces that come to us through them, for we need the poor just as much as — perhaps more so than — they may need us. If we are from affluent societies, helping the poor is our key to the heavenly mansions. "I was sick . . . Enter into the kingdom. . . ."

Catherine is always thinking about the life of Christ as a model for our life. So too here. She recalls that the Lord spent most of his earthly sojourn living our ordinary life. What will we do when we go to Pakistan or Africa? We just go and live the same kind of life we have been living in Combermere. We don't have any special program: *our way of life is the program*. It is a life of ordinariness, of simplicity, of sharing what we have with others.

We will incarnate ourselves and be born like a little child to a new civilization and to a new people who will be our people. Like Ruth of the Bible we will leave our country and our people and incarnate ourselves as much as is spiritually possible into the ways of the new country or new city or a new part of America or Canada. The whole process is gentle, never violent, never coming from one who thinks himself better than the one who teaches. Incarnation is our first step. It's another name for identification, but a more powerful one, one that can shake the foundation of the world, change it, restore it to the Christ whose incarnation is the motivation of our own. The process is long and tedious and painful; but we must change, in a way, into the Hindu we serve, into the African we serve, inasmuch as love will enable us to do so. Without any compromise with our Christian principles. This is a deep incarnation. It will require prayer and fasting, contemplation, silence, work, dying to self. (*Ibid.*)

Catherine's attitude is not that everyone in the world already believes in Christ in some "anonymous" way, and therefore it's unnecessary to speak about Jesus. No. But love, the work of the Holy Spirit, must *precede* the message, however it is finally communicated. In fact, only love will be able to find a way to communicate the Gospel in a life-giving way.

The Lord said to his apostles, "Go and make disciples of all nations." There weren't really nations at that time. The word used in the Gospel is closer to "cultures": "Go and purify all cultures and make disciples of all peoples living in those cultures."

A culture is like the clothes of a particular people — their customs, language, songs, art, how they express who they are. To preach the Gospel to them we must clothe ourselves in their skin, get inside their ways of life, rituals, dances, patterns of speaking and thinking. It is presumed that every marketplace needs to be purified by the Word.

In Nazareth Jesus was doing precisely that — clothing himself with our existence. He had taken our nature upon himself. He lived and walked around in our clothes for thirty years so that when he finally did speak and act he did so in ways the people could understand — in *their* ways. If he had been born in Brooklyn in 1930, he would have spoken and acted differently.

In Nazareth he listened to the particular cultural existence he had assumed — the language, the customs, the
thought patterns. And when he finally spoke, the simplest
people could understand him. He spoke about birds and
seed and catching men like fish. Anyone who was of the
truth was able to hear his voice and understand, and understanding, be converted and live.

In our own Nazareth — the community of love where
we are nourished — we get in touch with the marketplace of
our own hearts. This is the mystery of *kenosis*: we empty our
hearts of whatever prevents us from identifying with others.
Once we have heard the Gospel clearly in our own hearts, we
will be able to speak it clearly to others. The *kenosis* Catherine
speaks about leads to the freedom to be able to identify.
Then, because of the self-emptying, we are free to enter into
the marketplaces of the world. If we have learned to live the
Gospel in our own Nazareth, we will be able to go and live it
anywhere.

> There is no other way to enter into a people. Strangely
> enough, it does not consist in the poverty of rats, of mad
> dogs outside. It doesn't consist in drinking putrid water.
> No, it doesn't consist in any of those things. What happens
> is a mysterious thing. It's a mystery worked in the soul by
> God himself. It's the mystery of dying to self through
> others for love of him. It begins with compassion. If you
> never opened your mouth, never taught a lesson, never did
> anything but just *be there* the way you are, you would fulfill
> the great commandment to love God through your neigh-
> bor. It all leads to identification — you with God in the
> manger, [identifying] with his weakness and smallness and
> poverty and dependence.
>
> Of course your stay in the village is fruitful. The things that
> really matter in the apostolate, however, are not a matter of
> results. They have no other reason but love. Our vocation

is to love and often for years never to see any results; but always remembering that we are tillers of the soil. the ones who till it and make it ready for Christ to sow. He and he alone can give it a harvest.

THE TIME OF FRIENDSHIP, WORD AND SACRAMENT

Years ago Jacques Lowe's book, *As If He Had Seen the Invisible* spoke very much to Catherine's heart. He described three main phases of the Lord's sojourn among us: the time of friendship, his simple, ordinary life in Nazareth; the time of the Word, when he publicly spoke the good news; the time of the Sacrament, the three hours on the Cross. Catherine expands on these three phases and relates them to her own Gospel vision.

The time of friendship is Nazareth, the childhood presence, a life of shared working together, a thousand acquaintances, the bonds of kinship which make people say, "Is this not the carpenter, the Son of Joseph?"

Have you thought about this, the time of friendship for us in Madonna House? It's the time of the hidden life, the buried leaven, of silence that accepts cultural differences and difficulties, anything and everything. It is the blending of the missionaries with the people they serve. It's a time of uselessness, the secrecy of the Father. For he deals with missionaries as he dealt with his Son. He wants to send us into his Bethlehem and his Nazareth. Perhaps that is what I mean exactly when I talk about the chit-chat apostolate, I'm talking about this time of Nazareth and friendship.

THE CHIT-CHAT APOSTOLATE

There are many aspects to this life of Nazareth, this time of friendship among a people. But there is one aspect which, for Catherine, is a doorway to all the others, and the most characteristic feature of her approach to mission — the chit-chat apostolate:

> My technique has always been the chit-chat apostolate. I did not believe, by the grace of God and my own background, that we can do anything in a massive way, that is, by dealing with masses of people. I never went in for big meetings and so forth. Fr. Mulvoy in Harlem tried to involve me in such things but I said, "Oh, Father, you do that. I'll just meet the Negro person by person."
>
> Always I tend to put across this person-to-person approach. People are afraid to meet the other person. People are afraid to meet the Negro. People are afraid to meet local people. People are afraid to meet the hobo. People are afraid, and they draw back. People are afraid to talk to a little group of local people. People are afraid because they are afraid of being ridiculed, maybe laughed at.
>
> They will not produce great results. God wants that we should love everybody, that we should be free with the freedom of the children of God. God wants that we should be free to talk to everybody. That freedom is achieved by prayer. There is no other way to make us free except by prayer. I foresee that we must go to people person to person. That is the chit-chat apostolate that is going to be the solution of our apostolate. I mean the essence, not the solution. (SLFF #3, 1970)

There are several points worth emphasizing here. Being free of one's fears to approach others, person to person, is somehow the *essence of the apostolate* considered from the point of view of a missionary "technique." What changes people most of all is meeting someone who genuinely loves them. To do this we must overcome our fear of loving the other. This can only be achieved by *prayer* (which we will consider further on).

The ordinary approach of much apostolic activity is to immediately set up a program and begin helping people. This can bear certain fruits. But often this can be quite impersonal, the program getting in the way of the communication of personal love. Catherine's approach is to sit down with people and have a cup of coffee with them and get to know them first. That personal contact is the essence of the apostolate.

I have often heard people who were the beneficiaries of Catherine's apostolic activity remark that what affected them most was not the program but the impact of her personal love on them. They remember the power of her love, and it changed them forever. (Christ changed them, of course, but working through Catherine's personal love.) And many people who were formed by her twenty, thirty years ago, continue to lead fruitful Gospel lives. They had been set on fire, and they continue to light fires themselves. They were touched by the love of God in Catherine, and they were never quite the same afterwards.

It is also in keeping with her Gospel intuition that not only is such an individual approach necessary to radically change a person's life, but if you just change a few peoples' lives, you can change the world. She is not interested in approaching people en masse. She is interested in setting fire to one person at a time. It is such people who can then change others.

Many of the words of Christ in the New Testament were probably spoken only to his small band of disciples. He spent a great deal of time forming this little group. It seems his plan was that, if a few understood his teaching in some depth, then they could spread it to others, and eventually to the world. And they did.

Trotszky said once that with a hundred really dedicated people you could take over any country in the world. Catherine (who often spoke of the dedication of die-hard Communists), I'm sure, also believed that a small, dedicated band of people, totally in love with Christ could accomplish much.

"STAY WITH ME": THE POUSTINIA IN THE MARKETPLACE

The best explanation of what Catherine means by "staying with Christ in the marketplace" is to be found in her teaching on the "poustinia in the marketplace." (I will treat the poustinia further on. I can mention here that Catherine, in Combermere, in 1962, introduced the poustinia as a cabin, a place apart for solitude and prayer. "Poustinia" is the Russian word for "desert.")

The poustinia in the marketplace is one of Catherine's symbols for integration — the unity of prayer and action; retaining a wholeness in our hearts while pouring them out in service for others; our union with God while immersed in the pain of the world. It is her way of describing what she means by staying with the Lord in the marketplace. She recounts the birth of her insight concerning the poustinia in the marketplace.

> It happened during the visitation of one of our houses in 1968. One morning I was listening with my heart to the various reports being given. Portland House was very

involved in all kinds of things, good things. They were
involved with migrant workers, clothing rooms, study
groups, etc. I was suddenly shaken by a thought that had
never ever dimly entered my mind. I saw three people that
were being called to a poustinia in the marketplace. So, at
one point in the meeting, after the reports had been given,
there was a heavy silence. With that silence a bombshell
fell. Quite unexpectedly, almost without knowing what I
was saying, I put the following question to everyone:
"What if the Lord needs this house to be a poustinia in the
marketplace? This will be a new flowering for our apostolate, to be this presence in the marketplace." (P, 78)

It was a Pentecostal experience. Not one of us doubted it
was from the Holy Spirit. It came like a wind, like tongues
of fire that, though shaken, our silence had the quality of
awe and astonishment and fear; yet our hearts listened. In
some strange way we knew that this was the unity. It's what
I wanted to do in the beginning. (*Ibid.*)

Catherine's original vision of her vocation — "what she
wanted to do in the beginning" — was just to go into the
marketplace of the city and live a hidden life of prayer and
service to the poor. This Pentecostal experience narrated
above recalled her early longings. I say *her* longings because,
as she soon learned, *God* had other plans for her!

The "poustinia in the marketplace" was a new grace for
Catherine, revealing unsuspected depths of how to be immersed in service while keeping the spirit of her own Little
Mandate. In Combermere she had been led into the depths
of the life of Nazareth — a perfect community of love,
revealing on earth, as much as possible, the life of the
Blessed Trinity, the life of Jesus, Mary and Joseph. This
community existence *is* the preaching of the Gospel, *is* the

essence of mission. The new insight was to *now live this community of love in the midst of the marketplace*.

> It will be an intensification of your love for one another and your hearts open to everyone, revealing the face of Christ to them. Be careful, the devil will try above all to destroy your love for one another. The only thing that can destroy us is the lack of love. (*Ibid.*)

Speaking of this Portland experience years later, she wrote:

> It seemed that I had found some kind of connection between solitude and crowds, between fasting and feeding others. In a blinding instant, in a flash, it all came together. It was only a beginning. It was as if I grasped the edge of his garment. I sensed that if I could hold onto it, he would show himself in a strange dispossession. At that moment I realized that the memories that I outlined above [that is, about her original vocation of hiddenness] were footsteps in the sands of time that the Lord let me take, to lead myself and all of you to the poustinia. It's the answer of God to us. Something vitally important. (SLFF #3, 1970)

It is because of this new Pentecostal grace that the last houses Catherine established before she died were called listening houses, of which Portland was the first. In the later years of her life she said that "the chit-chat apostolate now is listening," which I think is very significant.

Catherine was always attuned to the needs of others. At one time *we* used to knock on doors. Now we are present in the marketplace, living the life of Nazareth, and people come and knock on *our* doors. It's the same person-to-person contact. The new but not exclusive emphasis was on tending the wound of loneliness in the modern cities. We

live our community life with a door always open to those
who need a listening heart.

God is at work in everyone. What allows the light of his
presence to shine in hearts is the power of love. "The form
of the apostolate doesn't matter." What matters is love. This
is not a teaching of indifference, that it doesn't matter if
people believe in Christ or not. Catherine believed that
Christ was the Savior of the world, and that it was the
Father's plan for all to come to believe in him.

But how are people to become aware of the light of
Christ shining within them? Through love. Where love is,
God is. Through kenosis we come to befriend the poor man
within, which each one of us is. Then we are free enough
from self to identify with the other. Identification leads to an
openness on the part of the other. And then, when the heart
has opened, Love can enter.

To many people viewing the latter part of Catherine's
life from outside the community, from outside of Combermere, and without knowing the new phases of her interior journey which happened there, it often seems that she
abandoned the marketplace and opted for a "counter-
culture life-style in the country." It is an understandable
evaluation — but quite superficial.

During the last 30 years of her life Catherine was led
into the depths of her vocation and vision. She had spent
many years in fighting for racial and social justice. But more
and more she intuited that the greatest need of our post-
Christian era was an authentic Catholic/Christian restoration of *the whole of culture*. She realized that not only was the
Gospel absent from racial or social issues; it was disappear-
ing from social life. Combermere is a tiny seed containing a
vision for the restoration of every aspect of human
existence.

In one sense there was a withdrawal from former types

of apostolate, but only so that God could lead Catherine into planting firmly the community of love, which then would become the source of all the apostolates of the future. God wanted to teach Catherine, and us through her, that the community of love is the primary apostolate; everything else is secondary.

It will be the task of her spiritual children to fashion new forms of the apostolate, based on, and flowing out of, the incredible depths of her own journey inward. No apostolate is foreign to us, but it must flow from the house of love. In a sense, she left us on the brink of this enterprise, poised and listening to the modern world, clothed for the journey in the risen Christ. Future forms of "going into the marketplace" are as yet hidden in the Hearts of Jesus and our Lady of Combermere.

CHAPTER TWO

Pray

Catherine always tried to live the gospel as literally as possible. She read there: "He told them a parable about the necessity of praying always, and of not giving up" (Lk 18, 1). And St. Paul instructed his disciples to "pray without ceasing" (1 Th 5, 17).

Like the Russian seeker in *The Way of a Pilgrim*, Catherine too is a Russian pilgrim of the Absolute searching for an understanding of this command of the Lord — "pray always."

Catherine, through the grace of God, really *did* achieve the magnificent state of "praying always", and her total teaching on the Christian life is capable of leading others to this goal also.

The injunction to pray occurs three times in the Mandate. Because it first appears in relation to going into the marketplace, I will consider prayer here in a more active sense: *to obtain strength to stay with Christ in the turmoil of the marketplace.* Then, in the last line, I will treat prayer in the more contemplative sense of resting in the Beloved wherever we are. In discussing this last line I will present the symbols Catherine uses for the integrated state of action and contemplation. As has been remarked, perhaps one way of envisioning the goal of the Mandate is to always be prayer-fully resting in the Beloved in the midst of the marketplace where Christ is both in anguish and gloriously risen.

I will present in this chapter her general teaching on prayer, and something of her own prayer journey. (It is always important to remember, when reflecting on Catherine's teachings, that she herself traveled a very long road to achieve union with her Beloved.)

Prayer is the conscious journey into God's Heart through a dialogue of love with him: "How can you define prayer except by saying that it is love? It is love expressed in speech, and love expressed in silence. To put it another way, prayer is the meeting of two loves: the love of God and our love. That's all there is to prayer." (SMS, 8)

A NEW BREED OF CONTEMPLATIVE

What follows is one of Catherine's best descriptions of what it means to pray in the marketplace, and the goal she desires for all her spiritual children:

I have been thinking about the spirit of our Institute as a whole. And one thought lingers with me that I want to share with you. That our apostolate, factually one of the most active that can be imagined by men, is destined by God, I think, to be deeply contemplative.

For how in heaven's name will we be able to face up for a lifetime — that is broken into small particles of days that will bring us doubts, temptations and fears! — I repeat: How in heaven's name will we stand up to that grind of those grains of sand that are such days, unless we become contemplatives? Unless we enter the immense silence of God and His soothing tranquility; unless we repose, rest on his breast, listening to no other sounds than the heartbeats of God that will reveal to us, in part at least, and in proportion to the depth of our silence and recollection, his love for us.

Yes, we are a new breed of contemplatives, whose monasteries and convents are busy streets of new pagan cities, noisy thoroughfares of immense metropolises that sing the hymns of the flesh, the world and the devil; of endless rural roads that would be God's if men who hate him or do not know him did not travel on them!

Yes, we are a new breed of contemplatives, whose prayer is accompanied by the noise of swishing cars and clanking bells, and tramping feet.

We are a new breed of contemplatives, whose bells are knocks at old dilapidated doors. Yes, we are a new breed of contemplatives who must learn repose, rest, on the breast of God, listening to the perfect music of his heartbeats whilst we go about his business and that of his Father, moving amongst one of the most broken-down, discordant, uneven, out-of-pitch music that the world ever heard. (SL #9, 1957)

"I have repeated ad infinitum, A LAY APOSTLE MUST BE A CONTEMPLATIVE. By this I always meant that our contemplation is done in the marketplace and, with a few exceptions of retreats, days of recollection, poustinias and prayer time, is and can only be done there, i.e., in the marketplace." (LDM, #196, Sept. 1965)

THE NECESSITY OF PRAYER

We cannot journey into the Lonely Christ, nor become aware of our being in the risen Christ, without prayer. And

all the fears we must overcome to enter God's Heart, our
Lady's Heart, our own heart, and the hearts of others,
cannot be accomplished without prayer. Just as in human
friendship we overcome our isolation and distance with one
another through conversation and deeper personal knowledge of the other, so it is with the Lord. The basic problem of
humanity is our disorientation, our distance in friendship,
from the Lord of life who made us and loves us. All fears —
the fear of God, of death, of ourselves, of others — can only
be radically overcome through the intimacy of prayer.
Prayer is the great key to union with God and freedom from
fear.

> How are we going to strip ourselves? Before God we are
> both resplendent, because we are created in his image and
> have his divine life, but at the same time we are paupers
> that have nothing of our own. So the answer is simple and
> very concrete: We must become contemplatives, that is to
> say, we must pray constantly, without ceasing. (SL 116,
> 1962)

> I see Christians the world over battling with themselves,
> with hope and with despair. I see them almost giving up
> and retreating. At these moments, I am not ashamed to say
> that I kneel down, or even prostrate myself flat on the
> floor, for I know that against this North Wind there is only
> one remedy, PRAYER. (R, April, 1966)

And to seminarians she writes:

> Prayer is your life. There you will find strength, faith, and
> fortitude, not only to persevere, but to become an alter
> Christus, which you were always meant to be. Prayer will
> make you a giant, running on the way to God. Do not
> neglect it. Do not allow even the best and holiest of works of
> mercy to become for you the heresy of good works, or to
> take you away from prayer. (DS, 6-69)

There is only one way to lead men to God and that is to teach them prayer, and to pray for them. So the real answer to all our modern problems, whatever they may be, are two hands like Moses standing on the mountain of faith, animated by love, and sustained by hope. There is no other answer!

If this happens, if this happens to one person, this grace, this charism to stand up there with uplifted hands like Moses, then the miracle of action will take place. It seems so strange that the prostration of prayer, or the dance of prayer, or the rock-stillness of prayer, or whatever form prayer takes, floods the world with action. Because he who turns his face to God in prayer, he who has been led to the summit to lift his hands and be still, seems also to be in the eye of the hurricane, the eye of action.

This, then, is the ultimate being of a Christian. We all must lead one another to the top of the mountain to pray, because prayer is dynamic, and prayer is holy. It is a contact with God; it is a union with him. When we do this, then indeed we have accepted his saying, we have fulfilled his invitation! Now we can act! (Unpub.Talk)

PRAYER IS SIMPLE

For Catherine, first of all, prayer is simple, not complicated:

Prayer is so very simple. Many people think it is something esoteric, as if you could learn to pray only after having studied theology and spirituality and all the different methodologies of prayer from St. Teresa of Avila to transcendental meditation! I think if Christ had wanted to talk to Ph.D.'s he would have found their equivalent in the

society of his day. He didn't. He talked to Peter and John.
He talked to illiterate people who didn't know how to read
or write, and they absorbed his voice and understood his
words because he spoke so simply. If you want to know
what prayer is, listen to a child of two or three. (SS, 7)

PRAYER A "RISKY BUSINESS"

One of the marks of the authenticity of Catherine's
spirituality is her realism about the cross. Many people today
confuse prayer with meditation exercises whereby they seek
to achieve peace or a state of mindlessness:

> In Zen Buddhism, one is supposed to sit in the lotus posi-
> tion and meditate until nothing at all is left in the mind:
> Forget about yesterday, today and tomorrow, and concen-
> trate on the present moment. But, it seems to me, Chris-
> tianity has a better idea. For us, contemplation is the con-
> templation of a Person. (SS, 11-12)

This comment by Catherine is of one piece with her
absolutely incarnational spirituality. Influenced by Bud-
dhist and Hindu approaches to meditation, there is a wide-
spread notion today that the more perfect goal of prayer is
not thinking or speaking to anyone. "Meditation" has come
to mean achieving peace by focusing on a beautiful land-
scape, or by gazing into the starry heavens, or by clearing the
mind of any thought whatsoever. For Catherine, prayer is
speaking with the Beloved. The traditional definition of
prayer as being "conversation with God" is how Catherine
understood it. It is nothing complicated, nothing new,
nothing requiring seminars to learn!
But the Scriptures and the lives of the saints — and also
Catherine's life — reveal that speaking with God, simple as it

may be, is a very demanding kind of conversation. He is the Lord of Lords, the King of Kings. We must be ready to hear and obey what he asks of us. He seeks to draw us beyond all our fears, and clasp us to his Heart. We must literally "fall" in love with God, fall into Love, fall without fear into his arms and allow his heartbeats to overpower us.

> In many books one has the impression that we should all learn to pray because prayer is so interesting and so thrilling, that it is the discovery of a new world where one meets God and finds the way to spiritual life. That is true, but the implications of prayer are more far-reaching than that. Prayer is an adventure, but it is a dangerous one. We cannot enter into it without risk. As St.Paul says, "It is a fearful thing to fall into the hands of the living God."

> At Madonna House, our experience with the poustinia, and with the million and one questions people ask, has shown us that we can't speak of prayer as if it were some new fad everyone should try. Prayer must lead us to total surrender, or it will lead us nowhere except back to ourselves.

> It is this surrender that we fear so much, and this is why prayer is such a fearsome and dangerous thing. This is why following Christ is indeed a risky business. He calls us to enter a revolution — not like the fight for a cause, but one that is infinitely more powerful. This revolution takes place inside of us, for heaven is taken by violence to *oneself.* Prayer is part of this adventure. Do not fool yourself: Once you encounter God, you will no longer be the same person you were before. (SS, 17-18)

FALLING IN LOVE WITH GOD

The great key to prayer is love — to love God by doing his will, and to love others through service. Prayer will deepen as our love deepens. It is by love that we penetrate into God's heart; and prayer will deepen our love for others.

Prayer will come when we fall in love with God. The way to fall in love with God is on our knees. Everything in us resists this falling in love. Who wants to fall in love with the Crucified One? But if we reach this point, prayer will spring like a song from our heart. Love will uphold it. When we fall in love with God we will receive the gift of compassion and tenderness. With these gifts, we will really begin to be people of the towel and the water, washing the feet of everyone, because now we know that everyone is Christ and Christ is in everyone. (SS 13)

But to love someone, I must know him. To know him, I must meet him. Then I will recognize him in others. How do I get to know Him, so that I can love Him and continue to love him in my brothers, and to love my brothers because I love Him? I know Him in prayer, prayer of all types. (R, Dec., 1968)

CATHERINE'S OWN PRAYER JOURNEY:
"MARY'S GARMENTS ARE TOO BIG"

Because Catherine speaks of prayer in many symbolic and poetic ways, we need to look briefly at her own journey to the state of praying always, which I believe she had achieved. We need to distinguish at least two phases of her long life of prayer.

We know from her diaries and correspondence that, in

her early years, she traveled the traditional road of prayer — daily Mass, prayer before the Blessed Sacrament, meditation time. In the latter part of her life she had achieved a true integration of prayer and life, the state of always resting in the arms of her Beloved while engaged in serving him in others. It was in this later stage of her life that she could say:

> When I think of prayer, the sentence that comes to me is this: "Hold the hand of the Lord, and talk to him any time you wish." There is not a time to pray and a time not to pray. To pray is to pray always. You hold the hand of God. Sometimes you talk to him and sometimes you don't, but you are with him all the time. That is what our basic approach to prayer must be.

> With so many people to pray for, long prayers are not necessary. That is why I simply say, "Lord, take care of so-and-so." I wish I could take each one of you by the hand and say, "Come with me. Let's all hold the hand of our Lord and pray in this simple fashion." Most of us are not used to praying as life flows along. We are used to spending so many hours in prayer. We are used to "taking time" for prayer, when, in truth, we should be praying all the time. Prayer never stops. It is such a beautiful thing to hold God's hand and to pray always. (SS, 21,23)

But Catherine did not *begin* her prayer walk in this integrated way. Around 1940, Father Paul Furfey, her spiritual director, began to call her to deeper prayer — contemplation even. Catherine struggled with this:

> No, Father, I still think you are mistaken. I still think God made me a Martha. I still think Mary's garments are way too big for me. What makes you think that I, so sinful and so weak, might even attempt the first steps on this royal

road of sanctity. . . . I haven't even an ounce of the contemplative in me, as I see it. (FF, 54, 57, 58).

But she continues to pray about it, and writes, not too long afterwards:

> Having faced this frightening picture [leadership in the Friendship House Movement] . . . I have come to the next point. If this is so that I must assume leadership then the answer is clear: I must do it. In order to do it well, I must throw myself on God more and more. The first thought that comes to me therefore is PRAYER, and ever more prayer. I do not mean only oral ones. No, mental prayer, meditation, contemplation even. Yes, Father, imagine: I who always was afraid of this word, I am willing now to embrace it if it is God's will. (Of course I realize that it is he who makes the first move; I only wait.) And especially the cultivation of God's presence through the day by short ejaculations and the lifting of my heart to him. I wait for your approval to begin this. Also, I think if you agree, I shall take a full hour in the afternoon before the Blessed Sacrament; heretofore it has been 30-45 minutes. The way I see it, PRAYER, then, or should I say *now*, becomes more and more imperative. (FL, 29)

A couple of years later she is making progress in prayer:

> Also a strange newness in praying and relationship to God . . . the prayer of petition seems unnecessary . . . nor is there any desire or inclination whatsoever to vocal prayer; nor even what I would have called, a few months ago, mental prayer. (FL, May 1, 1943)

> Deeper and deeper my thoughts probe into my own soul (all of this happens in the concentrated time of meditation and the silent time of contemplation. . . .) If it were not for

your insistence, I would never have gone in for these strange silent minutes . . . half hours and now almost hours of "just sitting there and looking at God . . . and letting him look at me." Are the deep thoughts that come to me his, or are they mine? (FL, April, 1944)

Father Furfey had challenged her to enter upon the road of contemplation. She was beginning to see more clearly that a contemplative presence to God was the heart of all activity: "What perverse trait is it in us that makes us look on Martha's work as important and on Mary's work as incidental? Yet, we all do make that mistake constantly. We think we are doing God's will when we are busy about many things. That's not the right way." (FL, 1941)

PRAYER AND SHARING CHRIST'S PAIN

We recall here Catherine's great theme of comforting Christ Who is in pain in the other in the marketplace. In the beautiful words of St. Augustine:

Christ's whole Body groans in pain. Until the end of the world when pain will pass away, this Man groans and cries to God. And each one of us has a part in that cry of the whole Body. In your day you cried out, and then your days passed away; another took your place and cried out in his day. You here, he there, and another there. The Body of Christ ceases not to cry out all the day, one member replacing the other whose voice is hushed. Thus there is but one Man who reaches unto the end of time, and those that cry out are always his members.

The groaning of *the Man* propels Catherine into the marketplace. The goal is "to listen to the perfect music of his heartbeats" even as we go about his business.

Stop . . . look . . . listen, and behold the pain of Christ! A
searing metal that should set your heart afire so that you
might both share His pain and become a flame that lights
and warms the world! Well may you ask at this point: How
do I propose you should do this, you who are walking in
that part of His vineyard that he has allotted you, and who
are assuaging His pain daily in hundreds of people? And
my answer comes to you simple and direct: LOVE MORE,
and to love more, PRAY MORE. Pray not only the prayers of
the Mass, the Hours, the rosary, spiritual reading, which,
of course, are essential, super-essential, the foundation of
all prayer. But pray the prayer of the presence of God. Ask
those who direct your soul to teach you. (SL 8, 1956)

Let us look briefly at the different kinds of prayer
Catherine herself practiced and taught to others.

"ALL CAN BE ENDURED BETWEEN
TWO MASSES"

One day Dom Virgil Michel, O.S.B., who was one of the
pioneers in the modern liturgical movement in America,
visited Friendship House in Toronto. The above phrase
about living between two Masses comes from him, and it
spoke powerfully to Catherine's heart:

All things can be endured and all things become possible
between two Masses: the Mass of yesterday and the Mass of
tomorrow. I need to be able to sustain one day of my life. I
need that Food if I am to live his commandments. I need
him daily because I am a sinner and weak. ("Daily Mass" in
Conquest, Winter, 1969-1970, p. 15)

Beautiful and simple is our prayer life that begins our day
with Mass . . . the Eucharist. What is there in heaven or

earth that can keep us from becoming contemplatives? For all lovers are contemplating the object of their love always and everywhere. So can we, in utter childlikeness and simplicity. To love is to contemplate. (SL #11, 1957)

If I stressed anything in my life it has always been the fact that liturgy — especially the Mass — is the very center of our life. You've got to implore God to help you. . . . Steep yourself in the Mass. Learn about it. Pray about it. For unless you do, your life in Madonna house will have no deep roots, no deep spiritual roots, and it might be one reason why your total surrender is being delayed so long. (SL, #118, 1962)

If any group of people need the Mass, we lay apostles of the marketplace do. We could not exist without it, nor persevere in our new, strange, and seemingly radical vocation of organized Catholic action. We could not even begin to try to practice the counsels of perfection, stability, and dedication . . . unless we daily came to the Food of the Poor Man. . . . Only in him, with him, and through him could we achieve our goal. (Unpub. Man.)

It is so simple. You have to pray to endure the monotony of those gray days. You have to pray. You have to pray without ceasing. Pray the Mass, of course. Always it is the center, the heart, the essence of our faith. It is the fire where you plunge to become its spark. It is your rendezvous with God. It is the only spot where you and Christ become one in the reality of faith and life. It is the meat that is going to keep you on the treadmill of those gray days, chained to the duty of the moment, chained without chains — for love is not a chain. (SL #140, 1956)

"JOINING WITH OUR BIG BROTHERS AND SISTERS IN RELIGION": THE LITURGY OF THE HOURS

Dom Virgil, in the early days of Friendship House in Toronto, also introduced Catherine to the canonical hours of Prime and Compline. She was thrilled to know that the laity also could pray these hours of the Divine Office. Ever afterwards she continued to incorporate several of the Hours into the daily schedule of her spiritual family. A humorous anecdote from the early Combermere days is recalled by Catherine:

> If Father Dwyer the Pastor were on time, we said Prime after Mass. If he were delayed, we said it before Mass. Altar boys spread the story that when Father Dwyer was late we said the Mass for him in the pews. If he were on time, we said Mass in the pews after he left. We killed that story, but it took us quite a little time! (HA, 509)

Many lay people now pray the Liturgy of the Hours. It is a wonderful way to be united daily with the whole Church as it prays and celebrates the mysteries of Christ. It is still an integral part of the Madonna House way of life.

"MOMENTS BEFORE HIS FACE": MEDITATION

"You are going to pray the prayer of meditation, in which your feet are going to run to and fro, and explore the life of him whom your heart loves, the mind of him whose will you desire to do with such a flaming desire because you are his." (SL #140, 1956)

"An oasis in the heat of our days are the moments spent before his Face and his tabernacle." (SL #11, 1957) As mentioned above, Catherine, in the early part of her pilgrimage, often spent an hour before the Blessed Sacrament each day.

THE "OPUS DEI" OF THE LAY APOSTLE

But we speak of God and contemplation of him, and it
might seem to us that after Mass that we haven't thought of
him for a single moment, until duty brought us back to
chapel. This is where our work begins, the real "Opus Dei"
of a lay apostle: we must begin to work on ourselves to
bring ourselves back to the contemplation of God. There
are many ways and means to help this travail of the soul.
Amongst them, if at all possible, half an hour before the
Blessed Sacrament in silent prayer during each 24 hours of
our lives. (SL #116, 1962)

An interesting expression here is the "Opus Dei" of the
lay apostle. "Opus Dei," the "work of God," is the traditional
monastic phrase for praying the Divine Office in common.
In the Rule of St. Benedict it is considered the main work of
the monk: "Let nothing be preferred to the work of God."
Catherine says that the lay person's constant struggle to be
mindful of the presence of the Beloved in the marketplace *is*
his or her "Opus Dei." You might say that to be able to
accomplish this "work of God" perfectly is also what she
means by constant prayer. "Opus Dei" is another of her
symbols for praying always.

THE NAME OF JESUS

"And then there is the prayer of the heart which repeats
the name of Jesus constantly." (SL #116, 1962)

Many in the West are becoming more and more familiar with the Jesus Prayer, "Lord Jesus Christ, Son of God,
have mercy on me, a sinner." This prayer is from the Eastern Orthodox tradition, and it is the basis for a whole school

of spirituality. Coming from Russia, Catherine was familiar with this prayer.

In Catherine's diaries we see that she had the practice of choosing a particular ejaculation, or short prayer, to say each the day. Ninety percent of the time her choice was simply the name of Jesus.

We presume, then, that she spoke this name thousands of times as she went about doing the will of her Beloved. It may be true to say that, for Catherine, the constant repeating of the name of Jesus, or "Jesus I love you," was her way of achieving and maintaining the goal of constant prayer, of constant awareness of the Beloved in the midst of service. What better way to achieve this awareness than using the Beloved's name!

The Eastern tradition teaches that one of the purposes of this prayer is to achieve an attentiveness to everything and everyone around you, noticing what needs to be done, the needs of the neighbor. This fruit of the Jesus Prayer would have fit in well with Catherine's desires for the marketplace.

> When you are in love, only one person matters to you, and that is your beloved. The others are just a crowd of people. When our beloved is God, we must recognize that he is the King, and we must surrender to him. The Jesus Prayer might be enough for us, "Lord Jesus Christ, Son of the living God, have mercy on me, a sinner." Why would it be enough? Because it brings Jesus into your life. The repetition of the holy Name brings the presence of the Person, for in the Hebrew tradition, the name of the person is the person. When I invoke the name of Jesus, I myself cease to exist. I am drawn into his name, immersed into his name, immersed in him. Once you've called on the name of Jesus, his name will remain with you because you desire it to be there too; and the two desires merge into one. (SS, 99-100)

POUSTINIA

Catherine's book *Poustinia* is already a modern spiritual classic, having been translated into half a dozen languages, and most recently into Japanese. Poustinia is the Russian word for "desert." One of the main thrusts of the book is a call to go apart into some room or cabin and spend time alone with the Lord.

As mentioned above, Catherine in her early life saw herself more as a Martha than as a Mary. But the Lord needed to teach her also the lessons of solitude:

"With all this comes only one thing that disturbs me: a craving for solitude. Though deep down I am alone with my God in the midst of turmoil around me, I dream of physically being alone. . . . Perhaps I must watch out here, for it might hurt this vocation of mine, which is active." (FL, 1941)

> What can help modern man find the answers to his own mystery and the mystery of him in whose image he is created . . . is silence, solitude — in a word, the desert. We need silence. . . . Yes, such silence is holy, a prayer beyond all prayers, leading to the final prayer of the constant presence of God, to the heights of contemplation. (P, 20-21)

> But broadly speaking, it amounted to a very simple affair. It amounted to seeking the Kingdom of God first within our souls; and then, when the noise outside becomes unbearable, and tension mounts, we should not be afraid to drop everything and go to the poustinia for 24, 36, or 48 hours. For we would easily do that — retire from action — if we had the flu or a temperature. How much more so for God? This was not an easy hurdle for members of this culture. For thousands of emotions reared themselves in our conversations, amongst them, guilt of not working. We agreed that this guilt must be slain at its roots by every possible means, natural and supernatural.

So the essence is to be before God all the time. And through the growth of love of God in man's soul, to develop an intuition as to when and how to drop everything that seems important, to regain a peace that is being lost. (LDM, Sept. 1965, #196)

I saw us going ALONE into our Poustinias, and I saw ourselves . . . trying to be totally dispossessed. And in that solitude of a room or a cabin, I suddenly saw the brotherhood of men under the Fatherhood of God take place in our own souls.

The Poustinia for me, at that moment, opened part of its secret! This was it: This life of prayer, solitude, fasting, led to true dispossession, and therefore to true identification! Identification with whom and with what? WITH CHRIST! If one gets identified with Christ, that means one gets identified with all men, and a strange mystery of God's dealing with man, and man's dealing with God, stood partly revealed before me at that moment during this July, 1972.

I admit that it rocked me. It was almost a traumatic experience. I seemed to have found some kind of a connection between solitude and crowds, between fasting and feeding others, between penance and joy. In a blinding instant and a flash it all came together. It was as if I grasped the edge of his garment. . . . (SLFF 11, 1972)

The "edge of His garment" was an insight into the relatedness of solitude to the marketplace. Solitude can help one become more dispossessed of the self, more identified with Christ, and therefore more concerned about and identified with everyone. We will see later that "Poustinia of the heart" is her symbolic phrase for living in the cell of your heart in the midst of the actual marketplace.

CHAPTER THREE

Fast

The mandate's prophetic call to fast occurs in the context of going into the marketplace and staying with the Lord. Although fasting has many dimensions, my focus will be to consider fasting as *a preparation for going into, and staying in,* the marketplace.

As is well known, the word "fasting" in the Scriptures has other meanings. Fasting in reference to *injustice* finds its classic expression in Isaiah 58:5-7: "Is that what you call fasting. . . . Is this not the sort of fast that pleases me . . . to break the unjust fetters and undo the thongs of the yoke, to let the oppressed go free, and break every yoke, to share your bread with the hungry and shelter the homeless poor." It would be difficult to express more clearly the apostolate of the marketplace.

Catherine, too, often used the word "fast" in this symbolic sense. But here I will treat fasting in its most literal sense as fasting from food. As such it is one of the spiritual weapons necessary in order to enter the depth of the marketplace.

It is extremely important to insist, however, that, for Catherine, as for the prophet, one of the primary purposes of fasting from food is the emptying of the false self so that we may be more free to minister to Christ in the poor. All our ascetical practices have love for their goal: "Abba Theonas said, 'We do not practice patience and love in order to fast, but we fast that we may succeed in attaining love and purity of heart' " (Cassian). The purpose of all ascetical practices is something positive — a purity of the spirit, a festival of the heart.

Food is not evil. One of the metaphors for heaven is the eternal banquet of the Lamb that will last forever. Having been exalted with Christ (*huphsos*), we are already seated with him at the heavenly table. But because our hearts are not yet pure, therefore must we fast. Fasting from food during our earthly pilgrimage is not an optional practice. The Lord said, "*When* you fast" (Mt 6:16), not "*if* you fast.

GOD'S WORD AS OUR FOOD

In the wilderness the Lord quoted to Satan the words of Dt 8:3: "Man does not live on bread alone but on every word that comes from the mouth of God." God's will, God's law, God's word -- in some very deep and real sense — was meant *to be our food*, as when Jesus said, "My food is to do the will of My Father."

In the Garden of Eden story the act of disobedience — doing our own will — is described in terms of reaching out for forbidden food. Instead of believing that God's will was our life, we believed the lie that we could have even more life by following our own desires. The most important purpose and effect of fasting, then, is to restore our freedom to hear the Word of God and *experience this Word as our most substantial food*.

One particular day, as I waited in a state of anticipation for Communion, I suddenly said to myself, "Catherine, every day you feed yourself with the Word! The Word can be eaten!"

It is as if the footsteps that Adam and Eve heard in the twilight move toward me, and I am absorbed by God, absorbed by the Word. We read in the Scriptures, "In the beginning was the Word." All that God the Father created he created through the Word. It staggers my imagination to think that the Word actually becomes one with me in this way, and I with It. It becomes part of me.

Depending on how completely I absorb It, I reflect It visibly, Its rays emanating from me. I eat the Word with a love and a passion that have no equal. Now the Word fills me to overflowing. Now you see its reflection in me. I become one with the Word. I eat so much so that I cease to exist. The Word absorbs me in this way because I am willing, because I say to God, "Let me dissolve before my death. Let me be filled with you, so that every step I take is your step, and every gesture I make is your gesture."

This is beyond abandonment, beyond kenosis, beyond anything I can describe. It is like the void in which one meets God. I have surrendered to the Word. I have eaten it. *I am filled.* Now the Word preaches through me. (SS, 94-95)

In the Book of Exodus, Moses prepared to receive the Commandments by fasting: "The Lord said to Moses, 'Put these words in writing, for they are the terms of the covenant I am making with you and with Israel.' He stayed there with the Lord for forty days and forty nights, eating and drinking nothing. He inscribed on the tablets the words of the Covenant" (34:27-28).

And Christ's own sojourn of forty days in the wilderness

is meant to recall this same extraordinary giving of the Word to mankind, only now the Lord's fasting is a preparation for the new and final Word of God to be definitively given to the world in his own Person.

Fasting, then, empties our heart so that we may be filled with the Word of God; increases our spiritual hunger so that our appetite for the Word is insatiable. Feeding upon the Word, we are changed and become, as it were, a walking Gospel of the Word to others. "Now the Word preaches through me," as Catherine expressed it. And the Word of God tells us mostly to care for the poor, the widow, and the orphan. Fasting opens us to hear the Lord crying out in the needs of the poor.

"Listen to the Spirit," listen to God's voice, is a line of the Mandate. The Holy Spirit of Jesus will "bring to our minds everything that the Lord has said to us." Fasting is one of the means to help us listen more completely to the inspirations of the Spirit, especially as we journey through the wilderness of the marketplace.

Huphsos — we have been exalted with him. This means that the total victory of Christ in the wilderness is within us. In our struggles with fasting and temptation we should believe ever more strongly that Christ has already conquered all the temptations of the body. *Huphsos* means that the victory over our bodily struggles has already been achieved.

In general, this is what Catherine means by fasting: "To fast means both to subdue and to alert our senses. They have to be subdued because they distract us too much from the one thing necessary, namely, turning our focus to God and to God alone. Perhaps 'subdue' isn't the most apt word. Perhaps 'direct' would be better. Fasting directs our whole person towards the Lord" (Restoration).

FASTING AS STRENGTH FOR THE MARKETPLACE

"I could only do this — enter the marketplace — if I prayed and fasted." (Tape on HMCB)

The marketplace is first of all the human heart itself. One day when the disciples were unsuccessfully trying to cast out demons from this marketplace, they asked the Lord why they were unable to do so. He said that certain kinds of demons can only be cast out "by prayer and fasting." These powerful weapons must be brought to bear on the demons within and without. It is a spiritual battle. The Lord emerged from his desert of prayer and fasting "in the power of the Holy Spirit" (Lk 4:4). Fasting helps to release within us this same power of the Spirit of Jesus for exorcising the demons of the marketplace.

" 'Lord, it's impossible [being in the marketplace].' Okay, that's the moment when you have to go and pray and fast. For it's impossible for man to do that. What else can you do but pray and fast so as to be armed with the strength of the Lord." (CLM)

Now comes the next paragraph, "Go into the market-place. . . ." Yes, these days, what my father used to say really must take place: "If you want to reach God you must lift the two arms of fasting and prayer."

In our days when everybody is catering to the appetites of the flesh; in our days when the senses rule as if they were God, it is time that we should fast as well as pray.

The Lord fasted quite a bit, and we should follow in his footsteps. He said to his apostles when they complained that they couldn't cast the devil out from someone, "This kind can be cast out only by prayer and fasting" (Mk 9:28).

> We who are of one mind and heart, who have held hands to
> walk in the darkness of this world to restore it, we must
> continue to do so in the marketplace, and stay in the
> marketplace and fast and pray. (Sob 95-96)

> Stand still, don't run away! Stand still! Such is what the
> writers in Eastern spirituality offer as a remedy against the
> temptations of the devil. They also recommend more fast-
> ing. . . . (P 112-13)

We have several aspects of Catherine's teaching here.
The two arms of prayer and fasting," refer to Moses praying
on the mountain. It is the classic example of the power of
prayer and fasting for the battle in the marketplace: "As
long as Moses kept his arms raised Israel had the advantage;
when he let his arms fall, the advantage went to Amalek" (Ex
17:11)

In many of the Church's documents on the importance
of the contemplative life, she uses this image of Moses in
testimony of her belief that prayer and fasting can help turn
the tide of the spiritual warfare on the plains. Catherine
often reminded us that the battle was spiritual — love
against hate, light against darkness. Such battles ultimately
can only be fought with spiritual weapons. Prayer and fasting bring the spiritual power of God to bear in the
marketplace:

> For what are we fighting against? We are fighting against
> powers and principalities. And these can only be exorcised
> by love in the name of the Father and of the Son and of the
> Holy Spirit. These powers thrive in darkness; evil lurks in
> darkness; darkness covers up so many sins. It is so easy to
> doubt, to sow discord, to plant anger against each other in
> the darkness. What will dispel darkness? One thing: love.
> (SMH, 1956)

"Fasting is a remedy against the temptations of the devil," said Catherine. The principal temptation of the devil is pride. "My strength is made perfect in weakness (2 Cor 12:9)," said the risen Lord to St. Paul. The biblical expression for fasting means "to humble one's soul." I humbled my soul with fasting" (Ps 35:13). Fasting fosters a state of "experienced weakness," which then increases our dependence on God's strength. True fasting can lead to humility.

Our body and its well-being is the closest thing to us! When we experience bodily weakness (and how often sickness, if accepted in the right spirit, can be a grace), we are driven to call upon God for aid. Fasting helps to undermine our false self-sufficiency. When fasting is practiced in the true spirit of faith, the power of God is released in us and sustains us. We then begin to live more truly by grace and not by mere will power or other false securities.

In the Scriptures as in the Mandate, prayer and fasting are intimately linked together. Fasting, because it deepens our experience of weakness and dependency, intensifies our prayer.

"There beside the river Ahava, I proclaimed a fast: we were to humble ourselves before our God and pray to him for a successful journey. . . . So we fasted, pleading with our God for this favor, and he answered our prayers" (Ezr 8:21, 23). "In each of the churches they appointed elders, and with prayer and fasting they commended them to the Lord in whom they had come to believe" (Ac 14:22-23). Prayer is most powerful when accompanied by fasting.

FASTING AS A SIGN OF WAITING AND MOURNING

Often in the Scriptures people fast when they wish to express their grief. "Then David took hold of his garments and tore them, and all the men with him did the same. They mourned and wept and fasted until the evening for Saul and his son Jonathan, for the people of the Lord and for the house of Israel, because they had fallen by the sword" (2 S 1:11-12).

"Jesus said to them, 'Can you expect the bridegroom's friends to fast while the bridegroom is with them? As long as they have the bridegroom with them, there can be no fasting. But the time will come when the bridegroom will be taken away from them, and on that day they will fast' " (Mk 2:19-20).

This latter text had a great significance for the origin of the Lenten fast. As the early Christians began more elaborate preparations for celebrating the Easter mysteries — waiting, as they believed, for the imminent coming of the Lord — they recalled that Jesus had said his disciples would fast when he was taken from them. Fasting was a means of reminding themselves that the Bridegroom was absent. It increased their longing for his coming.

As we have frequently noted, Catherine had a profound mystical intuition that the Lord continues to suffer in his Mystical Body. Her passion was to console him. Fasting, then, also takes on a certain state of commiseration with the Lord in his own mourning over the sins of the world. The Lord is "absent" from the lives of so many people. How can we fully rejoice in this life when so many still do not know and love the Lord?

The Lord has an infinite longing to be known and loved by all his people. Through fasting we enter more deeply into the Lord's desire for the glory of his Father and the coming of the kingdom. This longing, always suffused with the glory of God, is, to use a beautiful phrase from the Eastern Church, a "bright sadness," but a sadness nonetheless.

Christ is the One who experiences most of all the confusion and sacrilege of the marketplace. Through fasting we can identify with those sufferings. Christ, because he is always profoundly and completely joined to humanity, (and therefore is always "in the marketplace"), draws us also into his passionate concern. Fasting — this felt hunger — keeps alive in our hearts a compassion for the sufferings of the Lord in the marketplace.

IDENTIFICATION WITH THE POOR

We saw above, in our treatment of the marketplace, that we must empty ourselves as the Lord emptied himself, clothe ourselves in the skin and culture of others as he did, so as to be free enough to identify with those to whom we are sent. Just as fasting allows us to better hear the word of God, and directs our whole person towards the Lord, so it also allows us *to listen to God Who is always at work in others.* "This is a deep incarnation, and it will require much prayer, fasting, meditation, contemplation, and silence to achieve, as well as work and dying to self" (SL #117,1962).

Thousands of people die every day because of lack of food. (I think a child dies every minute from malnutrition.) When we are hungry, we are more in touch with the hungry. We are reminded that Christ is hungry in the poor, and that we shall be judged on how we responded to their needs. Bodily hunger increases our compassion and concern for the materially hungry.

Through fasting we can also grow in compassion for the "spiritually poor," namely, those responsible for much of the world's poverty. Fasting should remind us to pray for those who are in great spiritual danger because, by their policies and actions, they deprive the poor of their food or their land or their just wages. I pray more for those responsible for injustice than for the poor themselves. The poor are in the hands of God. I tremble at the spiritual state of those depriving the poor of food. The cries of the poor certainly reach the ear of the God of all mercy and consolation. The prayers of the unconcerned rich are a stench in the nostrils of God.

FASTING AS ATONEMENT

"It is to be remembered that you are going to the desert for the following reasons: to fast . . . so that you might give him Christ, to a world that is so hungry for him . . . to atone for your sins and those of others." (P 54-55) "The pilgrim's fasting is not only for himself. As all gifts of God, it is for others, to atone for all those who give in to all kinds of excesses, by drinking, smoking, eating. Yes, he understands now very clearly his role in helping Christ." (St 75)

"Atonement," is a foreign concept for many in the modern world. It simply means "at-one-ment." It means that we really are one body in the Lord. Just as in our physical body blood can rush from a healthy to a weak part, so in the Mystical Body, when one member is sick or sinful, our prayer and penance can flow into them, and "make up for what is lacking in the sufferings of Christ."

Especially in North America, the most materially prosperous region on the earth, how many people are overweight, surfeited with too much food? How many are sick in spirit as well as body through overeating? By fasting we can help to gain graces of restraint for them; by our example we can remind people that fasting is physically healthy as well as spiritually wholesome. By fasting we can help to restore oneness to the body.

To sum up, fasting is simply part of pilgrimaging, which is the great theme of the Mandate. It is part of the pilgrim's discipline as he journeys to the lonely Christ: "Then you also had to get a bag made out of linen. It crisscrossed your shoulders from left to right, very much like water bags. In it would be a loaf of black bread and a little salt. On the other shoulder, crisscrossing from right to left, would be a gourd of water." (St 29)

Fasting is one of the means to effect the self-emptying of the pilgrim so he can become more aware of the risen Christ's presence within, so this presence can radiate from him to others as he journeys. Fasting intensifies the power of prayer; prayer increases mercy and service. Fasting helps us keep Christ company in the marketplace:

> Fasting is the soul of prayer, mercy is the lifeblood of fasting. Let no one try to separate them; they cannot be separated. If you have only one of them or not all together, you have nothing. So if you pray, fast; if you fast, show mercy; if you want your petition to be heard, hear the petitions of others. If you do not close your ear to others, you open God's ear to yourself. (St. Peter Chrysologus)

CHAPTER FOUR

Be Hidden . . . Be A Light To Your Neighbor's Feet

We have just seen that the mandate calls us into the marketplace, which is first of all the human heart; but secondarily, into all the spheres of human activity. And now we are admonished to be hidden there. How is it possible to be hidden in the midst of the human condition? And how can one be a "hidden light"? The Christian life is a participation in the attitudes, powers and gifts of Christ — in his very Spirit, his divine life (1 Peter). The call to be simultaneously hidden and a light must correspond, then, in some way, to a dimension of the Christ-life. How is the Christian both hidden and a shining light? That is the mystery of this present line.

Isaiah 42:1-4 is one of the prophetic words most frequently applied to Jesus by the New Testament writers: "Lo! My servant whom I have chosen, my beloved, in whom my soul delights. He will not bawl or cry out, his voice is not heard in the streets, he will not break the crushed reed, or snuff the faltering wick. . . ." Strange words of "non-speaking" for one who is to "present judgment to the nations" (v. 2). Isaiah here expresses a hiddenness about the Messiah, and a delicacy.

The journey to the lonely and in the risen Christ is also a journey into the mystery of the hiddenness of Christ, who is the Light of the world but unknown to much of the world: "... but standing among you — *unknown to you* — is the one who is coming after me. . . ." (Jn. 1,26). And even to those who know Christ by faith, are not his depths still hidden from our eyes? To be a light *even though hidden*, is an aspect of Christ's existence in the world, and therefore an aspect of the life of his disciples.

In these modern days of "witnessing" and tele-vangelism and media coverage and "high profile" and "visibility" and everything that passes as "news," we don't often think of *hiddenness* as part of the Christian life. In our media-conscious world, *not to be known* is almost equivalent to not existing at all! Before reflecting on Catherine's understanding of this aspect of the Mandate, let us see what the Scriptures have to say about hiddenness in reference to the Lord's and his servants' activity.

A HIDDEN GOD

"They will say to you, O Israel, 'Only with you is God, there is no rival, no other God. Truly with you is the God Who hides himself, the God of Israel is Savior' " (Is 45:14-15).

Since we sinned and hid from God in the garden, we now sometimes experience *God hiding from us*, as being unknown. This is because of sin. In actuality, says St. Paul, God is not very far from any one of us, for "in him we live and move and have our being."

In many pagan religions there is a dim perception of some "high god." This "unknown, high God," dimly sensed by the pagans, had been fully revealed to Israel. Until the

Lord Jesus came, God remained "hidden" in the bosom of Israel. The revelation at the time was for its children and for them alone. Now, of course, the revelation of the Trinity is for the whole world.

But we can understand "be hidden" in the Mandate in the sense that we who are the light of the world (Mt 5:14) carry around within, as did Israel before us, the great secret of the revelation of the true God. We are in the marketplace with the hidden God within us. He hides himself within us, waiting for an opportunity to reveal himself through us. The "light to the neighbor's feet" that we are called to be is the light of Christ manifested through us: "I am the light of the world" (Jn 8:12).

One of the early Christian writers said that what the soul is to the body, that Christians are to the world. Jesus called us salt, the preservative element in the world (Mt 5:13). Are we not, then, also like that yeast hidden in the dough: "The kingdom of heaven is like yeast which a woman took and put (literally "hid") in a hundred pounds of flour till it was all leavened" (Mt 13:33)?

The Wisdom that Christ is, and whom we carry within us, is still hidden in the world: "And yet I do speak words of wisdom to those who are ripe for it, not a wisdom belonging to this passing age, nor to any of its governing powers which are declining to their end; I speak God's hidden wisdom, his secret foreordained from the very beginning, to bring us to our full glory" (1 Cor 2:7).

Christ has been God's secret, hidden since the beginning of the world. We carry this great secret treasure around within us:

"I who am less than the least of all God's people have been entrusted with this special grace, not only of proclaiming to the pagans the infinite treasure of Christ but also of manifesting how the mystery is to be carried out. Through all the ages, this has been kept hidden in God, the Creator of everything" (Ep 3:8-9).

"In all this Jesus spoke to the crowds in parables; indeed, he would never speak to them except in parables. This was to fulfill the prophecy: 'I will speak to you in parables, and expound things hidden from the foundation of the world' " (Ps 78:2) (Mt 13:35).

"I became the servant of the Church by virtue of the task assigned to me by God for your benefit: to deliver his word in full; to announce the mystery hidden for long ages and through many generations, but now disclosed to God's people, to whom it was his will to make it known — to make known how rich and glorious it is among all nations. The mystery is this: Christ in you, the hope of glory" (Col 1:25-27).

"I want you to know how greatly I exert myself for you and for those at Laodicea, and for all who have never seen me, that their hearts may be encouraged as they are knit together in love, to have all the riches of assured understanding and the knowledge of God's mystery, of Christ, in whom lie hidden all the treasures of wisdom and knowledge" (Col 2:1-3).

Just as in the Old Testament God was hidden from much of the religious experience of mankind, so even now the great revelation of God, Christ, is still hidden in the world — in us.

God does not wish to be hidden! He has spoken. He has entered the world through his Son *in order to be known and loved.* Christ wants to be discovered, but so many people are not looking for him. This is part of his loneliness — wanting to be known but not being sought by his people. One who desires to be known and is not known, is lonely. By being hidden, we share in his longing to be known. It is another way of sharing in his loneliness.

Hiddenness is, then, first of all, the "unknownness" of the Light of the world. We who carry this Light within us share also in his unknownness, his hiddenness. Until people are ready to receive the Light, we share in the hiddenness of Christ in the world.

HIDDENNESS AS PREPAREDNESS

Being *ready* is part of hiddenness. Paint on a pallet, a baton on the podium, a violin on its stand, each is waiting for the hand of the master, each unnoticed and hidden until picked up and used for his purposes.

Carrying within us the mystery of Christ, we are poised, ready to be used by God at any moment, like an arrow in a quiver: "Yahweh called me before I was born, from my mother's womb he called my name. He made my mouth a sharp sword, and kept me in the shadow of his hand. He made me a sharpened arrow, and hid me in his quiver. He said to me, you are my servant. . . ." (Is 49:1-3).

One of Catherine's favorite images for the members of Madonna House is from the First Book of Samuel. Arrows in a quiver, stones in a pouch — both are hidden, but ready to be used to slay giants:

> He took his stick in his hand, selected five smooth stones from the river bed and put them in his shepherd's bag, in his pouch; then, sling in hand, he walked towards the Philistine (17:40).

> And so, in everyday life, what do we expect of you, or rather, what does God expect of you? A great simplicity, an absolute naturalness, a humility as ordinary as the air. For who are we? In the line of apostles we are the smallest, the littlest. We are lay people — consecrated, dedicated — but

lay people. We are very small. Remember what I always say. David looked at Goliath and saw a brook. In the brook he saw little pebbles; and he had a childish slingshot. He bent down and picked up those pebbles, put them in his sling, and slew the mighty Goliath.

The Lord does likewise with us. David is a prefiguration of Christ. The Lord looked at the world and saw the Goliaths of darkness waxing strong and fat, plucking away from him the souls for which his Son died. Christ his Son, with the sling of his grace, bends down into the brook of life. He picks up little pebbles, you and me, to fix into His sling. What must we do as lay apostles? The little pebbles must just "be there." It is up to God to shoot!

Here is the hand of the Lord, and here are the pebbles. They were worked over by the water. They are shiny and ready. They lie still on the palm of God's hand. It is for Him to pick them up, put them into His divine sling, and shoot wherever He desires. That's all!

But oh! what goes into those tiny pebbles! Chastity, poverty, obedience, humility, simplicity, naturalness, death to self, and love. The pebbles lie still in the palm of God's hand, content just to rest there. (SL #140, 1956)

The hiddenness of those stones lying in David's pouch is also true of our hiddenness in Christ. At any given moment, if we are ready, the Holy Spirit can use us to reveal to someone the mystery hidden from all ages, Christ the Lord. Our task is to be ready. The Mandate prepares us for this task, and we wait, "hidden with Christ in God." Just as Christ in Nazareth could have been considered as waiting in a state of preparedness for his Father's call to public life, so too we wait for the Spirit's movement.

Small objects are often hidden, but just because they are

small doesn't mean they are not powerful! *Smallness* is also part of the mystery of hiddenness. How could such small objects topple a huge giant! Catherine believed that the spiritual giants of our day — unbelief, greed, pride — could only be conquered by the small but powerful pebbles of humble people living the Gospel of Christ's power, who alone can win the victory.

"WHOM GOD LOVES, HE HIDES"

There is a French saying, "Whom God loves, he hides." What does this mean? It can mean that God protects, by hiddenness, the graces we have received. Notoriety can often lead to pride; and pride can lead to ascribing graces to ourselves instead of to the Lord. Hiddenness keeps us focused on the Lord as the Giver of the graces. In this sense, hiddenness relates to the second line of the Mandate where we are called to be little, that is, humble.

The saying could also mean that God protects those he loves: "One thing I ask of the Lord, this I seek: that I should live in the Lord's house all the days of my life, to gaze on the beauty of the Lord and go into his temple. He shelters me in his cabin, on the day of trouble; he hides me deep within his tent; he sets me high on a rock" (Ps 27:4-5). God hides to protect.

There is a theme in the Fathers of the Church that the secrets of the Incarnation were kept hidden from the machinations of the devil: "The virginity of Mary, and her giving birth, were hidden from the prince of this world; as was also the death of the Lord. Three mysteries of a cry which were wrought in the stillness of God" (St. Ignatius of Antioch). St. Therese, the Little Flower, said she was going to remain so hidden that even the devil would not know what was going on within her. She embraced hiddenness mostly as a way of humility and purity of heart, but also as a protection from the devil. She was so skilled at this game of hiddenness that even her own Sisters did not know what they would be able to say about her when she died!

Does not the Lord, in his teachings about prayer, fasting, and almsgiving call us to hiddenness, to humility (Mt 6)? And this, no doubt, to keep our hearts pure: We are to close our doors to pray; not seek public acclaim in our penances; not let our left hand know what our right hand is doing as we go about helping others. Such hiddenness results from a desire that God shine forth, that he be glorified and not ourselves. The Lord said, "Let your light shine so that men may . . . *glorify your Father* in heaven" (Mt 5:16).

Hiddenness is a state we enter so that God may increase and we may decrease. It is a characteristic of trying to act purely for God and not out of pride, or for the acclaim or approval of others. Having been acclaimed by others, we will loose the reward of the Lord. But, more tragically, we will not have acted out of love for the Lord but out of love for ourselves. Nor is this hiddenness timidity. An athlete poised on the bench, ready, willing and able to spring into the game at a moment's notice, is not timid. He is waiting to be called.

HIDDENNESS AS HOPE

Isn't it true that most of life grows in hiddenness? The Lord spoke of the seed growing in the hiddenness of the earth, and the farmer not knowing how it grows. The baby grows in the hiddenness and darkness of the womb. Dreams and desires grow in our hearts; thoughts in our minds. The artist, the composer, the philosopher, creating in their solitudes — are not the beginnings of life almost always hidden from view?

Hiddenness in this sense is an act of hope, an act of reliance on God's power to bring forth life. The seed dying, the baby growing slowly, the artist creating in solitude, not knowing often what fruits his creation will have, hoping it will give life and beauty to the world.

An embracing of hiddenness is an act of reliance on God's power to bring forth life: "Only God can make things grow," says St. Paul. Hiddenness results from the desire that *God* shine forth and be glorified and not ourselves.

With this biblical background, we turn now to Catherine's understanding of hiddenness.

THE HIDDENNESS OF NAZARETH

Catherine's thoughts about hiddenness center around Nazareth. In a paragraph which sums up almost the whole Mandate, Catherine sees hiddenness as a way for light to illumine the path of others.

> I understood always — remember that human understanding is dim, very dim — but I understood always that by going to my Bethlehem, my Nazareth, by identifying myself with the poor, by living their life, by living the Gospel without compromise, by loving always, by remaining little, I would be hidden as Christ was hidden in Nazareth. And I considered Nazareth, at the time, to be the end-all and be-all and center of my vocation. For only by being hidden would I be a light to my neighbor's feet in the slums; and that all my fears would be taken away. I believed it."
> (HMCB, 25)

And thanks be to God we are still almost as hidden as the
life of the Holy Three was in Nazareth. Let us always wish
to remain hidden in one way or another. For ours is the
apostolate of the alleyways . . . of the lonely places . . . lonely
in more ways than one . . . of the world. (SL 34, 1958)

The spirit of Madonna House is the spirit of Nazareth.
Hidden. Humble. (SL 183)

One of the aspects of the Lord's life that amazed
Catherine most of all, and which she pondered endlessly,
was not only how God could be unknown in Nazareth for 30
years, but *why* he should have chosen this path. Thus her
tremendous journey to Christ is also a journey into the
mystery of this hiddenness of his earthly existence. I believe
that in some very deep and precise way Catherine was always
in "Nazareth" in her being before God.

We tend to equate effectiveness and having influence
with "popularity," and "being known." To have any influence in the world, it is thought, you must enter politics or the
public realm and start moving the world around. The modern world considers being unknown equivalent to being
without influence.

The mystery of Nazareth, among other things, means
that real effectiveness in the world is totally bound up with
union with God. I believe God could have saved the world by
remaining unknown if he had so desired. (And was he not
hidden to most of the world of his day?) It is not a question of
being known or unknown, *but of doing the Father's will.* Whoever is doing the Father's will is helping to heal the world. So
Catherine sought to enter this mystery of hiddenness, of
simply *being before the Father's face at all times.* If we could just
be in this sense, we would, by that very fact, be a light to the
world. To be a light you don't have to be a "big shot":

I always thought of Madonna House as small. I don't mean actually small as regards houses. (In Canada we had places in Toronto, Ottawa and Hamilton; in the U.S. we had Harlem, Chicago, and other places — seven altogether.) So in a sense it was big. But it was simple, exceedingly simple. It was humble, small, in the sense of unimportant; and certainly it didn't rate in the eyes of others. Let each staff worker have a heart wounded by the Lord, for the Lord, a poor heart, a humble heart, unpretentious, simple; a "no big-shot" deal. If this direction isn't followed, then there won't be a Madonna House. (MHWII, Ch. 29)

To do God's work does not mean to be "effective" in the worldly sense. The mystery of hiddenness means believing that your union with God is the important thing, not results. God asks us to be faithful to him, not effective or successful. The results depend on him:

Of course your stay in the village is fruitful. There is no need to give me any results or reasons. The things that really matter in the Apostolate show no results and have no other reason than love. There are results of your stay, but it is not given to you to see them, and that too is part of your vocation — *often for years never seeing any results*, always remembering that we are the tillers of the soil, the ones who plow it, make it ready for the Sower, and that He and He alone, through us alone, will sow it, and He alone will harvest it. [But] "a grain of wheat must die before it bears fruit."

Recognizing this hidden aspect of the work of Christ, Thomas Merton once wrote to Catherine:

Now, as always, God's real work remains obscure and humble in the eyes of the world. Now more than ever we have to be suspicious of results that are achieved by the efficient,

over-efficient technological means of which the world is so
proud. Christ works always humbly and almost in the dark,
but never more than now. I can think of nothing more
disquieting, more hopeless, than some of the supposedly
dazzling results of what is regarded as a Christian revival in
America. There may be some kind of a Christian revival
somewhere, but if there is one among us it is in the shade,
not in the limelight. (Personal Correspondence)

HIDDENNESS AS TRANSPARENCY

John the Baptist is an elusive character. This is due to
his transparency. He was only "a voice," a feeble word pointing to the Word. His life is a key to hiddenness as
transparency.

"John . . . who came as a witness to testify to the light, so
that through him all men might believe . . . only to testify to
the light. For he himself was not the light. The real Light
which gives light to every man was coming into the world"
(Jn 1:6). John was only a voice pointing to the true Light; he
was not the light himself.

In this sense there is a hiddenness, a transparency, even
about the Lord himself who always had his face turned
towards the Father. Perhaps his hiddenness in Nazareth was
due to his total absorption with the Father and the Father's
will. The Father told him to live in Nazareth. By doing this in
great simplicity and ordinariness, Jesus has become for all
ages a light for our ordinary days.

Hiddenness, therefore, does not simply mean being
unknown. It has more to do with being a window, a pointer,
an icon of something beyond the self. When we open the
curtains in the morning we rejoice in the sun and do not look

at the window. The window is there, but it is hidden, or rather, not seen, not attended to. It is only a medium for the light. By being totally centered on the Father's will in selfless love, we become transparent windows for the light of Christ:

> What is transparency? I see a window washed clean, through which whatever light is outside comes in, as if there were no window at all. If there is a sun outside such a window, it floods the room with its golden light, obliterating the window completely, because of its transparency.
>
> Is this Your way to unpollute the world? For if the soul itself, the person, was truly defenseless, forgiving, and loving, the result of this would be transparent minds, hearts and souls. A transparent soul would show You to everyone who seeks You, for unless we become transparent, people will not know You. For every human face is also an icon of Christ — so is every human heart. But for the icon to be reflected in the face, it must be painted in the hearts of men. (P, 163)

Next comes "Be hidden," and "Be a light to your neighbor's feet." Strange, paradoxical, contradictory statements. How shall I be hidden and yet be a light to my neighbor's feet? Very simply: Christ was hidden in Nazareth, and Nazareth is the light of many Christians, in fact, of all Christians. Charles de Foucauld founded his communities on Nazareth and on hiddenness, and we have so much in common with him. We started in the hidden places of the world — the slums — when it wasn't fashionable to be there. When we didn't have to be avant-garde.

Yes, our apostolate began in hiddenness, and continued in hiddenness; and yet, because it was hidden and still is, it is a light to many of our neighbors' feet. This is the strange, paradoxical way that God has of talking without speaking to the soul of man, in this case mine. This is the essence of the community of love. It is poor. It is childlike. It is little. It is simple. It listens to the Spirit. It doesn't seek publicity, as we moderns call it. It seeks hiddenness, and lo it becomes known. For when you hide yourself in humility, poverty, simplicity, childlikeness, a flame comes over you and over your house, and I think over Madonna House. A light of some sort that we do not see, but God makes others see. (COLM)

"When you hide yourself . . . a flame comes over you." An authentic spiritual life means you are aware that you are not the light, not the lamp. When you are more aware of the Light of Christ within you than of yourself, then, in some mysterious way, this Light radiates around you. On the other hand, if you are too preoccupied with *consciously being a light*, you get in the way of the true Light.

HIDDENNESS AS ORDINARINESS

Did you ever consider (maybe not, because they are so hidden!), that the most essential realities are often not consciously noticed, not attended to, but taken for granted?

You probably have not adverted to the white page upon which you are reading these words. Yet, without the white page, you would not be able to read. The white page is the light illuminating the words. We do not pay attention to the air we breath, the sun which shines, the ground upon which we walk. These realities are always present, giving sustenance, substance and light, as we go about our tasks.

In one of her commentaries on the Little Mandate concerning hiddenness, Catherine speaks about this theme of the *ordinary things which form a background for life*.

She recalled visiting a sick person on a farm. The priest

preceded her with the Blessed Sacrament; and in front of the priest was a boy with a lantern. "Now you see, nobody paid attention to that little light. It was so common to carry a lantern from your house to the barn. In a sense, the lantern was hidden. There are invisible men also." (LCom p. 12.) The invisible man she refers to here is the postman on his rounds whom no one sees because he is there all the time.

So, although she saw hiddenness *as a profound ordinariness*, it is an ordinariness which is essential for life to go on. The *hiddenness of essential realities*, you might say, is one of the aspects of life, and of the Christian life as well. It is a characteristic she desired for the apostolate.

In another place Catherine said, "To be truly hidden is to be totally revealed." (R Feb., 1971) When we are absorbed in the Father's will, we become "totally revealed," that is, simple, a light. Everyone is called to be concentrated on the Father's will in ordinary existence. It is at the heart of the Madonna House vocation and the Christian life:

"What is the vocation of Madonna House? First of all, terribly hidden, sometimes not making any sense at all. Yet, making an awesome sense both in the Church and in the secular world. Little things done well for the love of God . . . monotonous things, eternally repeated. . . ." (SLFF 23, 1973)

THE HIDDEN CROSS ILLUMINES

We have all experienced a sick person patiently bearing his or her suffering. When we enter such a person's presence does not he or she illumine our lives like a supernova? From contact with such a person we receive strength for our own suffering. We are edified and encouraged. Bearing our crosses patiently is another way of radiating, in a hidden fashion, the light of Christ and his peace:

> All of us have to carry the cross of the Lord. It is the one
> God has given us to go through to his resurrection. This is
> the one we should keep hidden. True, we can help to carry
> other people's crosses and they can help to carry our cros-
> ses, but the operative word here is "hidden." The Lord told
> us to give alms and fast in secret. Our very hiddenness
> becomes a light if we do not complain when we carry our
> crosses, if we carry our cross manfully, ready to help in the
> carrying of other people's crosses. Then we become a light
> to our neighbor's feet because we become an icon of Christ
> — shining! (So, 96-97)

The attitude of hiddenness does not impose one's cross on others, does not, by complaining, force others to help us carry our cross.

The word "complain" comes from the Latin word which means to "beat our breast in grief thoroughly." And here I mean complaining so that others can see! We don't mind suffering in a hidden manner as long as somebody eventually finds out about it! We don't mind being hidden, as long as we eventually become known! By bearing our crosses in a hidden manner we help to create peace around us. "For then indeed we are hidden and we are revealed as the men and women we should be . . . who pray for peace. . . ." (*Ibid.*)

HIDDENNESS AND LOVERS

Hiddenness is a characteristic of lovers: they seek hidden places to make love. This is why Jesus went apart to speak with his Father; this is why we go apart at times to speak to the Beloved. Love seeks hiddenness:

Arise and come once again . . . I am waiting. I am waiting on my heights, come. This is the "hidden place you dreamt of long ago when I first wove the fabric of your dreams.

This is the "hidden place," my Nazareth you wanted to share with Me so many years ago; when you did not know that I was sharing my passion with you. . . . (JI I, 149)

And in the final embrace, the Lord will speak to us the "hidden manna," which will be our new name, by which we are known to the Beloved alone (Rv 2:17).

JOY AS A LIGHT

For love to be a light it must be joyful. In a Christmas Letter of 1973 Catherine summed up the Gospel in a beautiful way:

Christianity is about the crucified Christ and the dancing Christ. We exist to wash the feet of men as Christ washed the feet of the apostles. This means entering into every phase of their life — spiritual, political, economic — and that means tension, anxiety, and a host of other emotions. But inside of our hearts *joy should sing*, for if our faith does not sing it is a kind of dead faith. For love is a song, the echo of God's voice, and we must make this echo available. We must make it heard by all those we come in contact with — for a song attracts more than a sob!

Joy is a way of washing the neighbor's feet, a way of being a light to the neighbor's feet. Christ, of course, consoles us more than we do him. The smile of the Babe of Bethlehem "will assuage our depressions, our anxieties, our tensions. From his smile we are going to learn to smile and sing ourselves. No matter where we are and what we have to do, we shall know that our life is an eternal pilgrimage to Bethlehem."

CHAPTER FIVE

Go Without Fears Into The Depths Of Men's Hearts . . . I Shall Be With You

GO

The journey into one's own heart is painful and crucifying enough. By the grace of God we do achieve some peace and freedom there through our acceptance of the gospel. But the mandate keeps calling us "to the poor," "to the market place," and now, in this line "into the depths of *men's* hearts."

The Mandate is not a call to rest, (except in the sense to be explained in the last line) — "I will be your rest." The Mandate is basically a constant summons to preach the Gospel — Christ — in all the hearts where people have not yet experienced him: "through love and being a light," to make others aware of his presence within them. While the final goal of the Mandate is union with the Heart of God, in this world the ideal is also the pilgrimage into human hearts, ushering people into the presence of the risen Christ. It is only by being "one with the poor," that we can be "one with the Lord."

And is it not also into human hearts that the prophets are told to go? "Speak to the heart of Jerusalem . . ." (Is 40:2); "The spirit of the Lord is upon me, the Lord has anointed me, he has sent me to bring the Good News to the poor, to bind up broken hearts . . ." (Is 61:1). This latter text the Lord himself used in the synagogue in Nazareth to describe his own mission, his own *going forth* into human hearts. What the poor need most of all — and remember, we are all poor — is the Good News of Jesus Christ. And this must be preached in human hearts.

This line — "Go without fears . . ." — occurs towards the end of the Mandate because the whole Mandate is a preparation for it. Catherine intimates as much when she writes:

> Of course, I had given away everything as he had asked me. The whole Mandate was there in my heart, as far as I was concerned. I had given up everything: I had gone to the poor; I had lived in the marketplace; I was poor with him and poor with them, and I hoped that all the things that the Mandate said were at least germinating in me, even though they hadn't attained full flowering. It takes a long while to attain such flowering. But I had begun. The Mandate said, "Go into the depths of men's hearts — I shall be with you." Well, that is another pilgrimage, and an important one. It doesn't apply only to me. It applies to everyone. (St, 52)

We should not attempt to go into a human heart unless we have achieved a certain humility, simplicity and childlikeness; in other words, until we have lived in Nazareth. Otherwise we will not be radiating the light of Christ but only spreading our own darkness and obscuring the Light. Unless we are united with Christ we will not understand that *only he really knows the human heart* and is able to heal it. Through hiddenness and humility, we become transparent for his light to shine in hearts.

The essential prerequisite for the journey into the hearts of others is, as we have seen, Catherine's call to journey into the mission field of our own heart. If we wish to understand the human heart, to radiate the light of the Gospel there, we must first realize the "tortuousness" of our own heart, and that God alone knows its depths:

> Tortuous is the heart more than anything, and desperately sick; who really knows it? I, the Lord, peer into the heart, and assay the innards of a man (Jr 17:9). You know every heart — You alone know the hearts of all mankind (1 K 8:40). The Almighty fathoms the Great Deep and the human heart, and he knows their designs (Si 42:18). God sees into the inmost parts of him, truly observes his heart (Ws 1:6). Sheol and Perdition lie open to the Lord, how much more the hearts of men (Pr 15:11).

And just as the Lord in Nazareth did not first of all *speak* but *listened* to the human heart and the human condition, so Catherine says that we do not first of all go into hearts to speak. She put it this way:

> When you talk about "going into the depths of men's hearts," it is not chit-chatting. It is not a question of discussing. It is strange and prayerful. To enter into men's hearts you don't necessarily talk to them. You *feel* them. You open yourself up, and it is a terrible thing. God permitted a Roman soldier to put a lance into his side. But he wants you to pull your rib cage apart, as it were, so that your heart is naked and that you really go into the depths of men's hearts. You cannot find out anything about those depths by cerebration. You can only find the depths by love, a love that tears you apart until there is nothing but little pieces left rotting in the sun.

It is entering into the very marrow of the other person. It is knowing without knowing what is to be done. It is like you were dead, and God discerns in you. I don't mean physically dead. I mean dead to the noise, to anything around you. You lie like one supine, like somebody hit you on the head or something. You hear and you don't hear; you see and you don't see.

And slowly, God takes you by the hand, deeper, deeper, deeper, until you reach the bottom. And then you can see into men's hearts from the other side — from God's side. Then he says, "Now you know. Act accordingly." You have to love with a love that transcends all understanding to do that. This is why your love is incomprehensible, because *you don't love, he loves.* (LDM, 1976)

This is a commentary on the truth that only God knows the human heart. To understand the human heart you must love, for love is a kind of knowing. It is the Holy Spirit of Christ "knowing" in you. If, through humility, you can listen to the human heart in this way, then and only then will you know what to do or say.

"THE ALMS OF WORDS"

Since the words of the Mandate are in the prophetic voice, and, since the prophet is told to "speak to the heart of Jerusalem," we too are called by the Spirit to give what Catherine refers to as the "alms of words."

The Word was made flesh and dwelt among us. The Uncreated became man for love of us. The Word of God walks among us, and yet millions in our dark and fearsome days "know him not." However, not only the fate of our own world and civilization, but also our life eternal depends upon our knowing and loving him. *It is therefore the accept-able time for us, the children of his light and love, to make him known.*

We can do this in many ways. The simplest and most direct way is through almsgiving. Not only can we give money, food and clothing . . . but we can give the alms of words which we all need. However, like all other alms, words must be given lovingly, gently, thoughtfully. To be able to dispense the alms of words, we must be one with the Word, and on the way to dying to self and living in him. One must try to see with his gentle eyes, think with his clear-sighted mind, try to love with his burning heart.

Do you see that lonely and sad child? Have you a moment to spare to give him the alms of a few little words? They will bring light into a darkness that should not be there. Making friends with a lonely, lost or unloved child, be he rich or poor, is to bring Christ into their hearts. And surely He will reverse the process in eternity by taking you into *his* heart!

A smile and a pleasant word to an ill-clad poor person in a public conveyance. How can we console the sick? How else but through the alms of our comforting words. The forgotten, the unwanted, the lost, the rambling alcoholic, the neurotic — would they be what they are if someone had given them the alms of words?

Such words of understanding, love, compassion, patience, and help are oils that soothe the burning wounds of exhausted minds. They are cool waters that quench the thirst that almost kills them. They are food that nourishes a starvation resembling that found in concentration camps. Words are often keys that open prison doors. They are so easy to give, yet so often withheld.

Everywhere, at all times of the night and day, people cry out for the alms of words. They cry silently not even

knowing why they cry. Yet they *do know* that they are
desperately hungry and thirsty for love and friendship. *But
love and its flower, friendship, are God, for God is Love, and Love
is the Word, and he clothed himself with flesh for love of us!*

Let us then lovingly show him to our brothers and sisters
expressed *in the thousand ways of love's ingenuity, but especially
in the alms of loving words!* (SL 114, 1962)

WITHOUT FEARS

If we have any knowledge at all of our own hearts we
know that it is a fearsome place. Jesus said that it is out of the
heart that lust, hatred and murder come (Lk 6:46; 15:18).
And was not the Lord referring to human hearts when he
used that frightful phrase, "The Son of Man is to be
betrayed into the hands of men" (Mk 26:45)?

Do we not fear the human heart more than anything
else? Isn't this why the prophets must constantly be encouraged to go and speak the message the Lord had given
them? Fear certainly does dominate our journey into human hearts. Although our faith tells us that every person is
the image and likeness of God, still, it requires much courage to enter "the land of souls."

"The Lord replied, 'Do not say "I am a child." Go to
whomever I send you, and speak whatever I command you.
Do not be afraid in their presence, for I am with you to
protect you. . . .' " (Jr 1:7-8). "Be strong, stand firm, have no
fear of them, no terror, for the Lord your God is going with
you; he will not fail you or desert you" (Dt 31:6).

"... go without fear." That's hard, because naturally we are
afraid to confront each other, aren't we? We're afraid to be
a path to each other, lest his feet might wear shoes with

nails. And so, at the last moment in our Little Mandate, when we have contemplated our fears — these fears notwithstanding — the Wind, the Fire, the Presence of Christ says to us, "Go without fears into the depths of men's hearts, I shall be with you." And suddenly, this Figure, seen darkly as in a glass, becomes luminously clear. If we let ourselves go, we shall rest in the hollow of His neck, as in the Song of Songs. (COM)

Fear of entering men's hearts is overcome by faith:

The mere thought of taking up Christ's cross and following him somewhere . . . nowhere . . . no place . . . is frightening, and when that fear gets hold of you your pilgrimage ceases. Fear is conquered by faith. Because your heart is faith-full, and because you love the God who calls you into the no-where . . . you go! Yes, we have to be faith-full to show the way, so we go.

THE VARIOUS FACES OF COURAGE

Fear is overcome by courage, which is derived from the Latin word for heart — "cor." Courage is having a great heart, a heart that is bigger than the fears, a heart that swallows up the fears in a greater love.

Courage does not consist in the absence of fear, fright, and worry, but in overcoming them for the sake of a greater good. The soldier on the battlefield is afraid, but he loves his country, and so he goes ahead courageously. The missionary who knows that his hour has come. . . . He is still afraid of pain. Mostly, however, he thinks about his soul, and prays to God to give him the flaming, fiery courage of the martyrs who went before him.

Perhaps we should begin in small ways to train ourselves to
grow in courage, to shed fear, to grow in faith and love of
God, a faith and love that humbly prays: "Lord, I am ready
to live and die for you, and I accept whatever form of death
your will has selected for me. But I am weak, and my soul is
housed in a house of clay. Be thou my strength, and give
me but one gift — the gift of perfect love of you that casts
out all fears."

Suffice to say that I learned slowly, as I hope you will, the
various faces of courage, which I repeat, is not the absence
of fear but the conquest of fear for a greater motive. (SL
#24, 1958)

I met a Black person once who had worked with
Catherine in Friendship House in the United States. She
said that "Catherine didn't know very much about Black
people when she went into Harlem in the late 30's, but she
went because she believed God was asking her to go. That
took tremendous courage. So *I know she is from God!*"

INTO THE DEPTHS OF MEN'S HEARTS
"GARDEN VARIETY LAY PEOPLE"

"Go without fear into the depths of men's hearts. I shall be
with you." What does it mean? You have all experienced it.
Who are we? Some of us have a little psychological
knowledge. Some of us are counsellors of a type. Some of
us have education. But the majority of us have nothing but
ourselves to offer. We are not counsellors. We are not
doctors of psychology. We are not psychiatrists. We are
ordinary, humble, "garden variety" lay people, with some
education, but not along these lines [of counselling].

Why do people invite us to go into their hearts? Why, in every one of our houses, do men and women, young and old, priests and nuns, "open their hearts to us?" Ask yourself that and you will know that it is because they see our poverty, our simplicity, and, I hope, our childlikeness. And they trust us, trust us to be good listeners to whom they really can "open their hearts." And God says to us, "Be not afraid. Listen. Enter those hearts. I shall be there waiting for you in them. And as I told you, be not afraid to speak what you have to say, because you will not be speaking, I will. Open your mouth and I shall speak." (COLM)

Catherine was not against learning and getting degrees in counseling. (Although, to my knowledge, no one in the community has ever gone away to obtain certification as a counselor.) She believed strongly that, if you loved God, then by that very fact, you were able to communicate that love. What people need most of all is a listening ear, and a confirmation that they are loved and accepted for who they are. This is how most healing takes place, and it cannot be taught.

This reminds me of a story about Catherine.

About a year or so before she died I was sitting with her in her cabin. She was in bed. I was asking her about her early days of nursing in the rural areas around Combermere. I said, "People must have been very glad to see you coming with your little black bag of medicine." "Oh," she said, "there wasn't very much in the bag. Life is mostly symbolic, you know."

My interpretation of that remark is this: Ninety-five percent of the healing was just going to see people, boiling some water on the stove, sitting down with them for an hour or so, perhaps holding their hand. What better medicine is there than that! We are all capable of doing this, and it doesn't require any degree. Such love creates a bridge over which we can walk into each others' hearts:

> If you are in love with God, passionately in love with God, and therefore vitally alerted to the needs and existence of your neighbor, you will make a bridge between yourself and him without any difficulty. For love seems to be a universally understood language.

> But the longer I live, the clearer I see that the answer to our personal, collective, national and international problems is bridge-making between human beings. Not allowing any human being to be an island unto himself, but connecting each with the other, with bridges of love. (R, March, 1963)

The present line of the Mandate we are considering is a call to have the courage to build such bridges.

HOSPITALITY OF THE HEART

> I speak of the hospitality of the heart as well as the hospitality of food and shelter.

> They come here usually hungry for God. This is their real reason for coming here, disguised under all kinds of other reasons. One thing they crave, whoever they are, and I sense it. It is as if somebody cried at the door and said to me: "Let me in! I have to touch someone who believes in God. I live in a desert of people who tear me apart. They talk about gods. They talk about what appears to be Antichrist. They talk about Satan. Everything in me is falling apart. I don't know any more what is right or wrong. Let me touch you. It is said that you know right from wrong, that you believe in God." This is the kind of real cry at our doorstep. If we are going to forget that then there is no need for any other kind of hospitality.

> The main point of our Apostolate everywhere is the hospitality of the heart. Our hospitality is an answer to peoples' hunger for God. It is through our hospitality that they will know love, care, gentleness, understanding, listening, etc. If we don't practice it, we might as well not have a library, or a PX, and so forth. Because all these things are there to feed a hungry heart through contact. (LDM, 1975)

If I had to choose the phrase which would sum up, best of all, the Mandate and the spirit of Madonna House, it would be this phrase — hospitality of the heart. Christ is present in others. He seeks a welcome, an acceptance. "I was lonely and you visited me." Through our own interior journey we become free enough, loving enough, to invite others to the feast, which is the presence of the risen Christ.

The following passage, from a manuscript Catherine wrote a few years before she died, describes, as well as anything she ever said, the essence of Madonna House, and therefore the essence of the Mandate. These are the opening paragraphs of the book:

> I am going to write "Madonna House — What Is It?" It Madonna House is based on hospitality, which is to open our door to anybody who knocks.

> But that is superficial hospitality. The pagans do likewise, as Christ himself said. There is the hospitality of the heart. How are we measuring up to the hospitality of the heart? It is an entirely different hospitality from the hospitality of an open door.

> When we begin to talk about the hospitality of the heart, we are talking about a wounded heart, at least that is how I see it. Yes, we are talking about a wounded heart, a heart that has been wounded by the love of God. A heart wounded by the knife of love, and of a passionate, incredible, God-given

love of himself. This can not happen by ourselves. It can only happen through prayer. He will give it to us. He will give us a wounded heart, a heart that has open doors always, and where others can rest.

It is said that Simeon, when he met our Lady, exclaimed, "A sword will pierce your heart." That is what I mean — a wounded heart. What is a wounded heart? A wounded heart is an open heart, completely open. It has only one gesture — arms wide open.

A wounded heart belongs to a crucified person. It is one who willingly and voluntarily moves up to the other side of the cross, opens his arms and says, "Put in the nails." A wounded heart is an open heart. It has no doors.

You begin to understand what a wounded heart is when you hear the Word of God which I repeat so often: "A new commandment I give you, that you love one another AS I HAVE LOVED YOU." He is not asking us to just love one another. He puts it straight: AS I HAVE LOVED YOU.

Now then, that is Madonna House. That is an open heart. We are not there yet. We are on the way, I'm sure. But I wish that somehow or other that wounded and open heart was really there so that when I come, weary and tired, even I who am a member of the place, could curl up and fall asleep in that wounded heart and rest myself.

A closed heart cannot say. "I'm open." I don't seem to be able to find anything that I could do to clarify all this. Yet, the charity of Christ urges me on. I want you to love him passionately, totally, completely, without ever turning back. That is the best I can do. You have to excuse me, but that is as far as my words go. (MHWII, Chap. 2)

Once I asked one of the family here what finally convinced her that this was her vocation. She said the very first day she got out of the car Catherine came out of the door and, with wide open arms, said, "Elizabeth, welcome home!" She said at that moment she knew she *had* come home.

And the final purpose of the Cross — "take up My cross" — is here revealed: it is to lance the heart so that others may come in; so that our hearts may become these inns for Christ in the other to find rest and welcome:

> People say, "What is Madonna House?" Madonna House is a very simple thing. It can be said in a few sentences. It is an open door. It is a cup of tea or coffee, warm or hot. Madonna House is a house of hospitality. It is a place where people are received, not on their education, not on how wonderful they are as painters or whatever they can do. They are received simply as people. They come and they go, and the memory of Madonna House lingers on. Something happens. What happens, nobody knows. But something happens. (SLFF 127, 1980)

The very first house Catherine opened she simply called, "Friendship House." She wanted to create a place where everyone would feel welcome, where people could meet as fellow pilgrims over a cup of tea. And the basis for this, she says in the same letter, is an acceptance of the fact that *we ourselves* are sinners: "God feels at home with us just because we are sinners, and because he came to save sinners. That is why God feels at home here. I want you to understand that.

Madonna House, in other words, is built on mercy, on acknowledging our own sinfulness. But Jesus loves sinners; he often came to eat with them. "Christ was very fond of sinners, of prostitutes, of unpleasant people, of all kinds of strange people. We are just that kind of people."

When we acknowledge our own need for Christ, he comes to visit us, feels comfortable in our homes. Then we can invite others and make them feel welcome also. Having been emptied of our pride by our own recognition of mercy, our hearts are now open to receive others who are in need.

And relating this to the previous theme, she shows how our *hiddenness* helps to make Christ feel at home: "It is your simplicity, your ordinariness, your duty of the moment, your non-desire to shine before men, that makes Christ at home in Madonna House. And where Christ is at home . . . others also feel at home."

Having made our own journey inward and become "at home with Christ," we are now able to create a place where others are at home also.

A PRECIPITOUS AND BLOODY JOURNEY

The constant presence of the cross is one of the signs of the Gospel authenticity of Catherine's vision: "If anyone wants to be my disciple, let him take up his cross . . ." says the Gospel; "Take up My cross . . ." says the Mandate. The journey into hearts is bloody:

> Yes, my feet were bloody because, quite evidently, I was still pilgrimaging. I was on a pilgrimage that was both outward and inward. Suddenly I knew why my feet were bloody: I was going into the depths of men's hearts. That is a precipitous pilgrimage. The depths are stony and they wound your feet. You walk on sharp gravel. You try to hold on to something but there is nothing to hold on to. So, when you go into men's hearts, your feet get bloody. (St, 51-52)

The hardest cross to carry is the descent into another's deep heart, to feel that heart, to be present not simply with food and shelter and external aids, but to enter into the inner chamber of another's heart to take their pain upon yourself:

> Why [is the descent into hearts so bloody]? Going into men's hearts is a precipitous descent because men's hearts are deep; it is taking the pain of men upon yourself. I suddenly realized that there was something much deeper and more profound in pilgrimage than just bloody feet. It was the carrying of another man's cross. Crosses have a way of biting into your shoulders and into your back. That's when I realized that I was still on a pilgrimage, though it wasn't the way I had thought about it. It was the way God had thought about it. I was *fulfilling the Little Mandate* [emphasis added] as God wished me to do. (*Ibid.*)

And, again, it is love, love, love, always love that must be the driving force:

> Such a pilgrimage can be undertaken only with love and not with any ordinary human love. Human love does not want precipitous descents into men's hearts. It doesn't want to have bloody feet. It doesn't want to have bloody backs and deep scars from other peoples' crosses. Men don't want that, but God does, and men in love with God can't help themselves. They have to embark on this pilgrimage. . . . (*Ibid.*)

You will recall that we pray and fast because only these spiritual weapons can conquer certain demons within. When you enter men's hearts you must be ready to face such demons:

> As one listens to all those screaming, whispering cries of despair, to those cries of hope that men bring to a pilgrimage, one becomes cognizant again of why his feet are bloody. Because he who enters the hearts of men enters a

new world. One cannot describe it geographically. One can
only describe it as an immense, new — totally new — land:
the land of God. The land where sometimes the battle of
Jesus Christ and the devil in the desert is repeated. So when
you enter the hearts of men, you might possibly be entering at the moment when the devil is tempting man in the
same way that he tempted Jesus Christ. So vast is the land
of souls, so immense is the land of hearts, that a pilgrim
must enter in the spirit of the Gospel. No wonder the feet
of the pilgrim are bloody, for the hearts of men are often
stony, fragmented stones, not easy to walk on. (St, 56)

"I SHALL BE WITH YOU"

The word of the Mandate "Go" is in the prophetic
voice; and, "I shall be with you" is the constant promise of
the Lord whenever he sends someone on a mission. "Moses
said to God, 'Who am I to go to Pharaoh and bring the sons
of Israel out of Egypt?' 'I shall be with you,' was the answer"
(Ex 3:12).

Like Moses, do we also not tremble each time we
approach the doorway of a human heart? Egypt is a symbol
of the flesh pots, of the place of slavery, of the marketplaces
where demons are worshipped. The human heart is capable
of all this. The Lord doesn't tell us very much about where
we are going, or what we will meet in the human heart. He
promises to be with us, and to guide and protect us with his
presence.

When we go into the depths of men's hearts in the
power of the Spirit we will experience the strength to carry
any cross we find there; we will find words on our lips that
we have not "thought of beforehand"; we will experience
that God is with us in that deep and awesome place. The

constant promise is, "Do not be afraid in their presence, for I
am with you to protect you" (Jr 1:7-8).

"YOU SEE YOUR BROTHER, YOU SEE GOD"

But there is another sense in which "I will be with you"
is realized. In the Gospel, and in the first line of the Mandate, the Lord identifies himself with the other. "Going to
the poor . . . being one with them . . . one with Me."
Catherine believed that one day the Mandate would lead to
the Face of the Beloved:

> As the years go by you shall see the Face of your Beloved.
> Slowly, the thousand and one faces that told you their
> story, that asked for help, will take on the shape of one
> Face. Then, slowly, very slowly, you will touch your Be-
> loved before you die. Always, at any time and in any place,
> we can embrace our Beloved . . . by embracing our neigh-
> bor. (SL #140, 1956)

There was a saying among the desert Fathers, "You see
your brother, you see God." The inspiration for this saying
is a fruit of their meditation on the passage in Genesis of
Jacob's meeting with his brother. Jacob was afraid to meet
Esau, and sent gifts ahead to placate him — "a whole camp
of gifts.But Esau ran to meet him, took him in his arms,
threw himself on his neck and wept as he kissed him." And
Jacob insisted his brother keep the gifts he had brought him,
"for in fact I have come into your presence as into the
presence of God" (Gn 33).

This is a very unusual statement indeed. You will remember that, the night before, Jacob had wrestled with

God, and "named the place Peniel, because I have seen God
face to face and have survived" (Gn 32).

I think of this story now in relation to going into men's
hearts. What a struggle it is! How fearful we are! And yet,
God was faithful to his promise to Jacob. His brother kissed
him and threw his arms around him. His very name "Jacob"
means someone who has struggled with God and man and
has prevailed (32:29).

This is the promise held out to each of us. Not necessar-
ily that we will be kissed and embraced by everyone (!), but
that we will be kissed and embraced by the Lord who awaits
us in every person — "the shape of one Face." And we
experience this "one Face" because we have descended into
our own heart and become aware of our oneness with
everyone:

> A man of prayer descends into his inmost heart, into his
> natural heart first, and thence into those depths that are no
> longer of the flesh. He then finds *his deep heart*, reaches the
> profound spiritual, metaphysical core of his being; and
> looking into it he sees that the existence of mankind is not
> something alien and extraneous to him but is inextricably
> bound up with his own existence. (Archimandrite Sofrony)

Catherine expressed this experience at the end of the
journey as the grace "to be everyone":

> I am the millions who seek him — and yet I found him.
> How can that be? Why must I live as if I were all others?
> What am I? Who am I? I know — I am everyone, because I
> love him, my Lord. I am everyone whom he loves, that is
> my agony. That is my ecstasy. That is who and what I am.
> To be everyone for love of him is to participate in the
> fullness of his passion. (JI, I)

While "metaphysically and actually," God and others and the self are distinct, at the end of the journey the "circumferences" of these realities *experientially* blend into one. Because of the pain of the world, we can never be free of his passion as long as this life lasts.

THE PILGRIMAGE INTO HEARTS AND IDENTIFICATION

What am I talking about? Let us say that you have living with you a down-and-out, broken down, selfish, self-centered, not too clean hobo, who doesn't want to do a stitch of work to repay your hospitality. There are many ways you can face this situation. You can decide that it is a good Lenten mortification to bear with him. That will be good, but that is far from perfect.

The next step would be to realize what terrible handicaps this man may have suffered from the beginning of his life. Try to make the pilgrimage of his life, and ask yourself what would have happened to you if you had been in his place. You see, you demand from us, your superiors, that we should always understand you, constantly help you and patiently bear with you. . . . Look into the depths of your hearts and answer that question. True or false? *If you ask us to make that pilgrimage into your lives, you should be able to do the same for the imaginary hobo.*

That would be good if you could do this, but it still would not be perfect. It would be perfect if you tore open your guts, so to speak, opened your heart wide, and out of love *became that hobo.* Love, empathy and grace would help you to do that. You would *become that hobo in your mind, actually.* This would be identification.

At times like this, I clearly see Christ in my neighbor, and you should too. I don't mean I see the face of the human Christ of the Gospels. The Russians portray the Trinity as fire, light and movement. *We can see Christ in our neighbor, become drawn to that light, that flame, that movement.* Then, by the grace of God and the Divine Light that is in us, we can love that gross, lazy, good-for-nothing hobo for whom this *Light, this Flame, this Movement became incarnate and died on the cross. This is what I call identification. Love alone can do that.* Only if *you become him* will you know his needs and be able to help him. How else can you know? You will only be guessing. (SL 129, 1963)

CHAPTER SIX

Pray Always

We come to the last sentence, "Pray always. I will be your rest." Now the Pauper who had nowhere to lay his head tells us that if we share his poverty, if we are little, if we are simple, if we are childlike, if we preach the gospel with our life and listen to his Spirit, he, the Pauper, will become our rest, for we will be poor together — God and us — and this we shall achieve by praying always. (COM)

So we arrive, finally, at the last line of the Mandate, after quite a long journey! Catherine has sought to follow the "Supreme Pilgrim, the loving Pilgrim, who descended from heaven to earth and returned from earth to heaven, thereby making us free. Free to love and serve. Free to undertake a pilgrimage of that sort." (St 14) Catherine always focused her spiritual eyes on the life of this Pilgrim, so as to walk the same path he walked. We do well, then, in the first place, to reflect on how the Supreme Pilgrim, Christ, ended his earthly days among us, so we may have a faith vision concerning the final stage of the Mandate.

DEATH IN THE MARKETPLACE

Jesus died *in the marketplace on the eve of the Sabbath, the day of rest, pouring out his whole being in love and sacrifice.* Even on the Cross he was "always with the Father," praying and communing with him. The Lord's own final hours were not "restful" in the ordinary sense of that word.

It is important here to mention the Lord's final days of his earthly existence because Catherine constantly called us to the "Hill of the Skull." The Mandate reveals this "Hill of the Skull" to be an ever greater and greater penetration of the marketplace, of hearts, of the poor; and all this while growing in prayer and communion with God.

The "rest" of this line is the *rest in God in the midst of human hearts, rest in the midst of the marketplace, rest in the midst of the poor.* But also, as we shall see, the mirror image of this "rest" is an ever greater realization of living in the risen Christ. The "rest" of perfect delight and peace in God is not for this life. That is waiting for us on the other side of death.

Recall that Jesus died on the eve of the Sabbath rest. "Rest" for him, on his final day, was to be in the midst of suffering humanity. In other words, the movement and goal of the Mandate is towards an ever deeper realization of meeting Christ in the midst of the suffering world. We must pass through this crucifixion to the definitive Easter. This is our faith. In this world we are called to ever greater and greater love, prayer and service, growing, all the while, in an awareness of being in the risen Christ. To live in this paradoxical existence is our preparation for entry into eternal life. *Jesus in the marketplace on the Cross praying* — this is the faith reality for this final line.

"Why are you learning all these different ways of praying? First, to get the strength to stand still on the palm of God's hand, to lie still; secondly, to someday reach that *simple prayer of the presence of God* where in faith you possess him, whom tomorrow you shall possess in the reality of life eternal. It will come." (SL #140, 1956)

"Tomorrow," in eternity, will be the final possession, the everlasting rest. Now is the time for work and service. For Catherine, in this life, she only finds rest in the midst of living the Gospel.

The final years of her own life also bear this out. Her last books portray her own ever-increasing identification with a world in grave danger. In a sense, her prophetic outcries intensified during her final years:

> I lifted my voice and I told them: "Stop it! Don't do it! Don't put into action your arms, which are made for the destruction of the world. Look! In the midst of your airplanes, missiles, and submarines stands an enormous cross. It is as big as the sky. It loses itself in the universe. The transverse beams touch unknown areas. It comes from the hearts of men. See how it goes up and up and up, to the feet of the Father. How its shadow falls on the whole world. Don't do it! Don't annihilate! Don't kill! It is against the commandments of God, the loving God who died for us.
>
> My voice rose like thunder, but no one paid any attention to it." (U, 48)

And physically as well, she suffered a great deal during her last illness, offering all especially for the Church. She finally did become the "poor woman" she so ardently desired. Although physically she was removed from much of the world's turmoil, her spiritual identification only increased. She certainly died *on the cross in the marketplace*, as we who witnessed it can testify. She had reached a spiritual state of identification with the world in pain.

However, there is one essential difference between

Jesus' state and ours: On the cross he was not yet living his resurrected life, *while we do live in this resurrected life.* Our whole journey takes place *in the resurrected Christ,* and the resurrected Christ is the final goal.

The phrases I have underlined in the following text all refer to this intuition and vision of finding rest, of living in the resurrection (which is already the reality of eternal life in God), in the midst of the struggles of life. It is a commentary on this last line of the Mandate:

> . . . *no matter what state we are in,* if we let ourselves go, we shall rest in the hollow of His neck. That's in the Song of Songs; and that's where he adds, "I will be your rest."

> Resting in the arms of God is having one's ears opened by God. All this doesn't happen in a day. Like himself, *we must walk in the heat of a Palestinian day.* Like himself, *we have to go through everything he did.* But we know something that no-body else knew in his day. We know that we live in his resurrection, and that *he will temper this heat, and quiet the wind of our emotional storms* if we let him. (COM)

"We know that we live in his resurrection." *Catherine equates "rest" with her living in the resurrected life.* Although we still have our death to pass through — the wind and the heat — even now we live in the resurrected life.

PRAY ALWAYS: THE SYMBOLS OF A FULLY INTEGRATED CHRISTIAN LIFE

We have seen something of Catherine's own prayer journey — how she took time out for prayer and meditation in her early years. But, eventually, I believe she did achieve a total integration of life and prayer. It is to this total integration which she constantly calls us:

> Yes, we are a new breed of contemplatives who must learn repose, rest, on the breast of God — listening to the perfect music of His heartbeats — whilst we go about his business and that of his Father, moving amidst some of the most broken down, discordant, uneven, out-of-pitch music that the world has ever heard. (SL 9, 1957)

She used various *symbolic phrases* to express this integration: contemplatives in repose in the midst of the Father's business; prayer is work and work is prayer; "being a prayer"; "the poustinia of the heart"; "being before God"; to "stand before God while walking with men." They all express, from different Gospel perspectives, the desire for, and living experience of, always being aware of the Beloved's presence no matter what one is doing:

> Now, people can be busy while still keeping the people they love present to them. A woman can be a nurse, taking care of her patients with great efficiency; yet, in her mind and heart be deeply united with her husband . . . the eyes of her heart behold the countenance of her beloved. What human beings can do when they love one another, a Christian can do with the Tremendous Lover who is the Lord. (GWC, 123)

I will treat, therefore, in this chapter, her symbols of integration, her symbolic phrases for praying always. Then, in a final chapter, I will treat the phrase "I will be your rest."

"BECOMING A PRAYER"

What is said next about "being a prayer" will apply as well to all the other symbols of integration. "Being a prayer" is the symbol Catherine elaborates the most, and so serves as a profound description of what an integrated life means.

In our "Way of Life" we read: "A cruciform man is a symbol of prayer. For no one will be crucified unless HE IS A PRAYER. No one will have the strength to be crucified unless God gives him the strength. God gives it to those who are 'prayers,' and I mean 'prayers.' For clothing the Gospel with our flesh means that we have to BECOME A PRAYER BEFORE GOD." In other words, when you are crucified with Christ, you are a prayer; when you live the Gospel completely, you have become a prayer.

In the following passage she reveals something extremely important about her own prayer journey. She says simply that she arrived at an integration of life and prayer *by meditating on the Gospel*. "Becoming a prayer" means perfect identification with the words of the Beloved.

> I proceeded slowly, even painstakingly, to vocal prayers. Suddenly those were left behind, and I found myself in a new land — the land of meditation. I always compare it to going to a dance and finding a boy friend who deeply attracts you. You remember and savor every word he says. My Lover was Christ, and so I read the Gospel avidly, meditating on each word. The Gospel became my favorite prayer.

> But the land of meditation was also a temporary one. Meditation fell away as old clothes, and now I was clad in the beautiful garments of contemplation. Life was entirely different now. It seemed as if the Lord himself were explaining things to me. In meditation, my intellect had

sought the answers. Now God himself clarified this or that
passage. I was lost in God in those days.

Where does one go after being "lost in God"? The answer is
a strange one, difficult to understand. You will not be able
to understand it with your head, only with your heart.
What happened now was that *I myself became a prayer.* (SMS
25-26)

"Becoming a prayer" means you have arrived at some
stage of love whereby activity no longer distracts you from
the Beloved:

A person who is a prayer is someone deeply in love with the
Word. He is deeply in love with a Person. When you are in
love with God, your head is plunged into your heart. It is
the happiest time of your life. Of course, we use our minds
as far as practical needs are concerned. The house gets
cleaned. The duty of the moment is always there. Far from
interfering with your life, "being a prayer" makes you very
meticulous about doing little things well for the love of
God. The detached, critical part of your brain that endlessly dissects and analyzes and reasons about matters of
faith has gone into your heart. This is what it means to
become a prayer. (26)

This perfection of prayer leads to the *identification with
Christ in the other*, one of the goals of the Mandate:

Prayer is suffering. It is com-passion. Suddenly, out of
nowhere, the suffering of humanity will fill you and you
are like one dead. You listen to the news, and you are the
man who has been kidnapped by terrorists. You become
the woman dying of cancer. Sometimes you go into the
depths of hell, a man-made hell, an atheistic hell. You
identify with the atheist. But you descended there of your

own free will, out of love. The pain of the whole world is
upon you. At this moment you don't "pray." You simply
share the suffering. That is what it means to be a prayer.
(26,27)

Being a prayer is not only an experience of suffering or
identification with those in pain. It is also identification with
those who rejoice:

From another corner of the earth, you hear good news!
You hear of a fiesta being celebrated, and you share the
happiness! Suddenly you feel like dancing in the middle of
the night. You feel that perhaps God is dancing with you.
Yes, you are becoming a prayer. (27)

And, even when we can't pray, St.Paul tell us that the
Spirit is praying in us; and is this not constant prayer:
"You can't pray? God sits there and doesn't mind at all.
He prays for you (Rm 8:26). As you pray about the living,
the suffering, the doubting, and all manner of things, God is
there. Once he is there, all things are there, and you become
a prayer." (27) Just as we have already been "exalted with
Christ" (*huphsos*) to the Father's right hand, so too, in the
risen Christ, we are already "prayers" because we are joined
to Christ who is "always interceding for us."
This integration of life and prayer — becoming a
prayer — is possible because of the Incarnation:

The mystery of God becoming man and of our humanity
"becoming God" meet in prayer: the prayer of the Son to
the Father, and our prayer to our Brother. At this point,
the mystery of being a prayer is more fully revealed. By his
Incarnation, the God-Man was able to pray to the Father,
and by our divinization in Christ, we are able to pray
through Jesus Christ to God the Father. God and human

beings are thus united in prayer, joined in the one prayer which is Jesus Christ. In him, we, too, become a prayer. (28)

Just as St. Paul said that Jesus is our "Yes" to God, so Catherine is saying that Jesus himself *is Prayer*, the Son whose whole being is love speaking love to the Father. In him our deepest being is already a total yes to God. The Christian journey is getting rid of all the noes!

THE "POUSTINIA OF THE HEART"

This is a symbol for the constant awareness of the presence of the Beloved within.

> When you come right down to it, the poustinia is not a place at all — and yet it is. It is a state, a vocation, belonging to all Christians by Baptism. *It is the vocation to be a contemplative.*

> There will always be solitaries, or should be. But the essence of the poustinia is that it is a place within oneself, a result of Baptism, where each of us contemplates the Trinity. Within my heart, within me, I am or should be constantly in the presence of God. This is another way of saying that I am a garden enclosed, where I walk and talk with God, where all in me is silent and where I am immersed in the silence of God. How stumbling the words are! How inadequate the similes! Yet the poustinia is something like this to me: a state of contemplating God in silence.

> The poustinia is a state of constantly being in the presence of God because one desires him with a great desire, because in him alone can one rest. My life of service and love to my fellowman is simply the echo of this silence and solitude.

For some people, this poustinia of the heart will take on, through the call of God, a definite physical dimension. But it is the poustinia of the heart that I believe is the answer for the modern world. This demands a kenosis. The kenosis begins with the repeating of the Jesus prayer. It begins with a silencing of the noise of my heart. It begins by my folding the wings of the intellect and putting my head into my heart. Only then will the poustinia of the heart become a reality.

Then indeed I can go anywhere, speak to anybody, make a community of love with my brothers and sisters, meet the stranger (who is simply a friend I haven't met yet).

Now it is not I doing these things, it is Christ within me. My words are not my own. They are the echoes of God's voice that comes to me out of his silence. Now I know how to catch fire from his words and become a fire myself, shedding sparks over the face of the earth. Now I can say that it is not I who live, but Christ lives in me. (P, 212-215)

The following poem, written during a very special year in Catherine's spiritual growth, expresses her entrance into the world of contemplation, the "garden enclosed," the poustinia of the heart, the experience out of which she now lives. The constant experiencing of the "kiss of his mouth" does not distract her from "the will of the Lord":

CHRIST WAS NIGH

The Lord called me suddenly out of the marketplace where I was busy about his Father's business. Yes, the Lord called me suddenly out of the marketplace and the heat of the day. He called me suddenly into his shade, and then into his glory.

But I did not arise and go as I should have done at once when the Lord spoke. For I looked at my garments and saw them as they were — soiled and in tatters from the sweat and the labors of the marketplace, from the heat of the day and the labor of the night.

No, I did not arise and go at once, for I saw more. I saw my soul covered with the leprosy of sins, many sins, sins forgiven and shriven. I saw my soul still covered with scars, the white, shining scars that the leprosy of sin leaves always behind.

No, I did not arise and go as I should have, in answer to the call of the Lord! I held back for an instant called time. Held back because I saw myself as my Lord's Father sees me, and I was sorely afraid!

But my Lord bent down, down to the thing of ugliness, sweat and scars that I was. Yes, the Lord bent down, down, and lifted my face into his cupped hands, kissed me with the kiss of his mouth.

And I became as white as the new fallen snow, and all my scars vanished beneath the touch of his lips. And my youth was renewed, and beauty shone forth from me. For I became clothed with the kiss of his mouth.

Then I arose from the depths of the marketplace, and I left the heat of the day behind me. I became a garden enclosed in a walled city. And the Lord shut the door of the garden that is I and took the keys away.

Now I am all his, a garden enclosed where he takes delight whenever he wishes. For now he is my Beloved, a seal upon my heart; and my mouth forever knows the kiss of his mouth, and my breasts the touch of his hand.

I am his garden enclosed! I lie in the sun of his passion, or in the night of his love, always. Now the will of my Lord is mine, and I have no other! (MHI, 6-7)

"WORK IS PRAYER AND PRAYER IS WORK"

We have seen, in a former chapter, something of Catherine's own prayer journey. This will now enable us to understand more clearly what Catherine meant by the phrase "work is prayer and prayer is work." (Note that she also says "prayer is work" — when you are praying you are also working.)

It is clear that this is another phrase for the total integration of life and prayer towards which she is always striving. It would be a mistake to understand this phrase as a kind of "substitution" of one for the other. For many years, until the last years of her life, Catherine spent one day a week in the physical poustinia, in prayer and penance.

Also, whenever Catherine wrote on this topic she entitled her letters with the Benedictine phrase, "Ora et Labora," (SLFF 128), which means prayer *and* work. And in another place she wrote, "Ora et labora dominates the spirit of Madonna House" (SLFF #129, 1980). The following passages make it clear that the phrase "work is prayer" is another symbol for integration, now from the point of view of *doing God's will each moment in a spirit of thanksgiving and self-offering.*

> In my life, to work and to pray factually meant the same thing, for all work of human hands and human intellect is a gift from God to man and from man to God. There should be no separation between work and prayer, for in this sense, PRAYER IS WORK, or should be, and he who

works, prays; that's the way it should be. In my personal life it was. It was called by my parents, "the duty of the moment is the duty of God!" Even to this day I have not strayed from this wonderful training that they gave me.

Time passed. My parents died. Fifty years ago I founded Friendship House and later Madonna House, in various towns of Canada and the U.S.A. One thing I remember, remember deeply — PRAYER AND WORK ARE INSEPARABLE. Or to put it in another way, "THE DUTY OF THE MOMENT IS THE DUTY OF GOD." And I followed this on a sometimes twisted, sometimes straight road of God's will. (SLFF #128, 1980)

When she was a young girl she often went with her mother to help the poor in their homes. She relates a conversation she had on one occasion with some poor Russian children in their house. She (Catherine) was explaining to them how this work that she and her mother were doing was prayer:

Then we got into a serious conversation, and I was expounding to them as best I could that work is prayer and prayer is work. The oldest boy who was about fourteen said to me: "Why do you talk about it? It is obvious, isn't it? You offer everything you have from God to God. That's all you have to do because everything that you have comes from him, and so you really have nothing. Since you have nothing, the only thing you can do is offer your world with love for him, and also your prayers. And since most of the people have to work very hard on the farm and elsewhere, well, all you have to do is offer God that work wrapped in a prayer.

"You know something," he said to me (and this I did *not* know at all), "when you do that, there is an angel who comes around and he really picks up both your prayer and your work and takes it straight up to heaven. It all depends on what kind of work you do. If it is woman's work, he gives it to Our Lady. If it is man's work, he gives it to Our Father, who art in heaven." He stopped talking, but I didn't stop listening. This was a novel idea. But then the Russians have a lot of imagination, so you have to take it perhaps with a grain of salt; but then, perhaps not. (*Ibid.*)

Catherine also had a "lot of imagination"! I believe she put into this story her basic idea behind "prayer is work." We belong entirely to God, so everything we have and are and do is to be offered to him. It is the early Christian intuition, expressed by St. Peter, that we are now "living stones making a spiritual house as a holy priesthood to offer the spiritual sacrifices made acceptable to God through Jesus Christ" (1 P 2:5).

Catherine equates "prayer is work" with the "duty of the moment," that is, with *doing God's will.* When we are doing God's will, the angels take our sacrifice to God, just as at the liturgy they take the Eucharistic sacrifice before the throne of God — "We pray that Your angel may take this sacrifice to Your altar in heaven. . . ."

This phrase, then, is a symbol of integration from the point of view of doing God's will. If you are not doing God's will, your work is not a prayer; or "if there is anger against God, then work is not a prayer" (*Ibid.*). As she said in the last line of the poem quoted above, "now the will of the Lord is mine, and I have no other." This phrase — "work is prayer" — expresses the perfect carrying out of the Lord's will. When you do that to some degree of perfection, an integration of life and prayer has been achieved. Then "your work is prayer."

NAZARETH AND "BEING BEFORE
GOD BEING"

"Being before God" is another of Catherine's symbolic phrase for praying always from the point of view of doing the Father's will: when you are doing the Father's will you are praying always; you as "being before God."

Jesus said, "Remain in my love. If you obey my commands you will remain in my love, just as I have obeyed my Father's commands and remain in his love" (Jn 15:9-10). "Remaining in the Father's love" is "being before God," and we remain — we most profoundly *are* — when we do the Father's will.

Catherine presents the life of the Holy Family as an example of truly "being before God":

There is no denying that Mary, God's Mother, was a contemplative. First and foremost She WAS ALWAYS BEFORE GOD. She lived in his presence, the presence of God the Father, of God the Holy Spirit, who overshadowed her, and of God the Son, who was bodily with her! Yet SHE WORKED FOR THE LORD TOO, serving the needs of Joseph and Jesus, and, I am certain, of many, many of the villagers. . . .

Joseph likewise was a contemplative. How could he be anything else? He lived with God and God's Mother. Yet one feels that he too "worked for the Lord," first by being a provider for his own family, and surely by assisting his neighbors. . . .

As to Christ himself!! BEING BEFORE HIS FATHER WAS HIS VERY LIFE! The very essence of it. DOING THE WILL OF HIS FATHER WAS ALSO THE ESSENCE OF HIS EXIST-

ENCE. What a simple answer I find here to the complexity
of the questions you asked of me. (SL #183, 1965)

In Christ alone do we have the complete integration of
prayer and life: Christ's work and being were one and the
same.

MARY, OUR LADY OF COMBERMERE

Catherine always had an extraordinary understanding
of the place of Mary in the Christian life. Born on the Feast
of Mary's Assumption, Catherine believed that Madonna
House, the House of Our Lady, was part of the Father's plan
in the modern world to restore Mary to her rightful place in
the hearts of her children. Catherine believed that Madonna
House had been given into Mary's hands by Her Son to do
with whatever she wished. And we believe the same.

Whatever decline in devotion to Mary in our tragic
times, we can say absolutely that such neglect is not the mind
of the Church, not the mind of God. In this century Mary
has continued to appear to her children on numerous occasions. The Second Vatican Council, in the document on the
Church, has reaffirmed our whole Marian tradition. And, in
his magnificent encyclical "The Mother of the Redeemer,"
Pope John Paul II has given us an unparalleled vision of
Mary's role in the Christian life.

Furthermore, in several post-conciliar documents, the
Church has directed that Catholic education on all levels be
integrated with the Marian dimension. Mary, then, must
become an integral part of the life of every Christian. This is
the teaching of the Church.

Mary is seen by Catherine as a model of the life of
prayer: she of all people was a prayer. I will say a few words

about Mary under the title by which she is invoked in our Madonna House family, Our Lady of Combermere.

The following poem expresses well who Our Lady of Combermere is:

> I am the Lady of Combermere. It is my wish that you make clear the meaning of my name to all the little ones so dear to me. To all who come to Combermere aflame with love of me.
>
> I am the Lady of Combermere. I am the Mother of the heights and depths of love. The Mother of the Valley high above the lowly haunts of men.
>
> No one can come to me without ascending, and none can reach these heights without descending into lowly nothingness.
>
> Heights are low and depths are high at Combermere. All weakness here is strength, and those who know how weak they are are those who grow in grace and power.
>
> I am the Lady of Combermere. My home is built on heights of lowliness and lighted with lamps of emptiness, and filled with wondrous sights of loveliness that those alone can see who walk in darkness and in me.
>
> The atmosphere is clear at Combermere, and clearest when the night is done and early morning mist is rising slowly with the rising sun.
>
> This is the valley where all sorrow is a joy, and all the painful crosses, happiness. This is where a winding river pauses to become my bay — the place where Love's tomorrow flows into today — so dear is Combermere to me, so near my heart, so much a part of our Triune Home in heaven.

I am the Lady of Combermere. I am the Mother of the
Valley high above the crumbling mountains and the falling
stars of all the loveless love in man. I am the Mother of the
Heights and Depths of Love — the Mother of my Son, the
God of Love Incarnate. (Unpub. Man.)

On June 8, 1960, Bishop William Smith, then bishop of
Pembroke, came to bless the statue of Our Lady of Combermere designed by the American artist Frances Rich. On
that occasion he said:

This afternoon in this very blessed part of the diocese, in
this very beautiful part of the world, in this month of June,
I know that, as the years go by, great graces will flow out all
over this diocese, all over Canada and the United States,
and all over the rest of the world through Our Lady of
Combermere. . . . In blessing the statue of Our Lady of
Combermere . . . I have in mind the thought that a great
deal of the work necessary to bring the world to the feet of
Our Lady will depend on the loyalty and devotion of the
friends of Combermere. Now we bless and dedicate the
diocese, and the country, and all the Americas to Our Lady
of Combermere. Graces will go out in abundance from Our
Lady of Combermere, and we shall all benefit from this
center of the lay apostolate . . . all of us . . . we in the diocese
and those outside. (R, July, 1960)

ST. JOSEPH

Our Blessed Lady was without sin. St. Joseph, as the
foster-father of Christ, spouse of the Virgin, and Patron of
the Universal Church, must also have received many extra-

ordinary graces. As we are considering here the final integration of the Christian life, it is appropriate to also say a few words about Joseph. He must have achieved a rare degree of union with God, of prayer and integration of life.

Joseph, as well as Mary, was involved in forming Jesus in his human experience. Joseph taught him how to walk, how to work, how to pray. He taught him how to speak: the vocabulary the Lord eventually used in his teaching came as much from Joseph as from Mary.

We associate Joseph with silence — "he passes through the whole of Scripture without speaking a word," says Paul Claudel. Joseph instructs us in the ways of silence so we can meditate on what the Lord has spoken to us. Joseph teaches us about the Fatherhood of God, just as Jesus received his human understanding of father from him.

After Mary, Joseph was the first to see the Incarnate Word in the flesh. He was chosen to be foster father because of his fidelity. God looked down on the earth and said, "Now, to whom can I entrust my Son, the Savior of the world, and his mother." An awesome assignment! Joseph teaches us the mysteries of fidelity.

And, in an age when there is a crisis in masculinity and manhood, Joseph can again teach men about true masculinity and fatherhood. (I think it was Peguy who said that "the revolutionaries of the 20th century will be the fathers of Christian families.") Joseph can teach us how to incarnate again, in families, the image of God the Father. Joseph is the patron of the laymen of our apostolate.

A prayer by Catherine describes very well her sentiments towards him:

> St. Joseph, you who know the silence of the night, the
> thickness of its dark that presses down mind and heart,
> keep me close. You who knew the size and shape of doubts,

and felt its sharp claws tear your mind. You who walked under the crushing weight, keep me close.

You who knew the haste of flight, and who felt the thousand fears that the slightest noises bring, keep me close. You who knew the desire, burning bright like flames, to put between you and those who pursue the frontiers of time and space, keep me close. You who drank the cup of exile and loneliness beyond all reckoning, and yet contained the bitterness and tears within the holy silence of your heart, keep me close.

St. Joseph, who died in the arms of the Lord, and so in death were within Life, tell me the secret of its night, and how far it would be for me to travel from death to life; and will you make the journey with me?

Oh, keep me close, St. Joseph, young and strong and alive. Tell me, what was it like in that holy night? Were the walls like gold, the stable walls, and was the straw like a thousand lights; or was it just like straw? And did he cry, or did you hear the music of creation near? Was the stable quite small, or did it grow immense and tall? Take me by the hand and show me where it stands.

St. Joseph, man of strength and wisdom and silence that speaks so loud, teach me to bear all wrongs in silence deep. Teach me to slacken my loneliness that cries like a child, night after night, at some hidden and holy stream.

St. Joseph, I know you understand these things, the hunger and the dream: the hunger that no one it seems feeds on earth; the dreams a woman can never share with anyone on earth. You understand. Keep me close! (Unpub. Man.)

CHAPTER SEVEN

I Will Be Your Rest

We all know what physical rest is! After a hard day's work, or streneous exercise, we flop down in our favorite chair, close our eyes, and relax. This is not the rest of the last line of the Mandate! The promise "I will be your rest" occurs as an effect, a result, a reward, the fulfillment of a promise connected with the command to pray always.

And we have seen that praying always is not the cessation of activity but rather the journey to the perfection of prayer and work, solitude and community, being and doing. The "rest" of the last line is living in the eye of the hurricane of the Blessed Trinity who is Light and Fire and Movement. It is precisely *in the midst of intense life in Christ* that the promise of his being our rest is fulfilled.

Note that the promise is *not that God will give us rest, but that he himself will be our rest* — *"I will be your rest."* What does it mean that even in this life God is our rest? That is the mystery we explore in this last line of the Mandate. It is a profound biblical concept. A brief consideration of this theme in Scripture will lead us into Catherine's understanding.

THE SABBATH AND THE PROMISED LAND

The notion of "rest" in the Bible applies to two realities: the Sabbath and the Promised Land. We will understand the Sabbath here as the *integration of the Christian life* I spoke of above. Rest is what we do after having achieved a goal. In this sense, the "poustinia of the heart," the "being before God," is the Sabbath for us.

The Promised Land is entering into possession of that which God has promised. In this life, it is the awareness and tranquil joy of possessing Jesus the Beloved in faith. I say, "in this life," because the Mandate concerns this life, and this last line concerns the faith awareness of the Beloved as we arrive at the perfection of spiritual integration.

Let us look briefly at some of the scriptural texts:

> Thus were completed the heavens and the earth with all their array. God finished on the seventh day the work he had done; on the seventh day he rested from the work he had done (Gn 2:1-3).

> Remember the Sabbath day and keep it holy. For in six days the Lord made the heavens and the earth and the sea and all that these hold, but on the seventh day he rested (Ex 20:8, 11).

Now when God rested he did not cease from "work": As the Lord says, "My Father works until now, and so do I." God's rest is (to speak symbolically) a deeper dimension of his activity. So too, the poustinia of the heart is not a cessation of spiritual activity but rather a perfection of it, and as such a completion, a "rest," in the biblical sense.

In commenting on the feast of the Sabbath, St. Thomas Aquinas says:

> All the solemnities of the Old Law were instituted to com-
> memorate a divine gift, either recalling one in the past or
> prefiguring one in the future. Among all the divine gifts of
> the past which should be borne in mind, the first and
> greatest is the gift of creation which is commemorated in
> keeping holy the Sabbath as the text in Exodus 20:11
> points out. Among all the future gifts which should be
> borne in mind the greatest and the final gift is the rest of
> the human spirit in God, either in the present by the gift of
> grace or in the future by the gift of glory; and this is
> symbolized by the keeping of the Sabbath.

The state of integration symbolized by the poustinia of the heart is the gift of grace, the intense sharing in God's own life. When we enter this state we enter the "rest of the human spirit," which is not physical rest but possession of God in faith.

"The Lord said to Moses, 'Speak to the sons of Israel and say to them: "You must keep my Sabbaths carefully, because the Sabbath is a sign between myself and you from generation to generation to show that it is I, the Lord, who make you holy" ' " (Ex 31:12).

When we arrive at some degree of perfection of integration, of being and doing, of working and praying, we will know that it was the Lord who brought us to this state. *This state itself is a sign of God's power in our lives as well as a celebration and a resting — a Sabbath.*

This state of integration will occur when the Lord has subdued all our enemies: "So it was the Lord gave the Israelites all the land he had sworn to give their fathers. They took possession of it and settled there. And the Lord gave them rest from all their enemies round about . . ." (Jos 21:43).

In a marvelous text on this passage, Origen says:

> This text was not accomplished except in Jesus Christ alone, who is my Lord. For if you think about yourself, you who have come to Jesus and from him through the grace of baptism have received forgiveness of your sins, so that now there is in you no war of the flesh against the spirit and the spirit against the flesh, then your land is at rest from war; provided that you bear about in your body the death of Jesus, so that as all battles cease within you, you become a peacemaker and are called a child of God.

Catherine would have loved this text! Even in the state of rest we bear about in our bodies the death of Jesus. But then we become peacemakers, bridge-builders, and repossess our birthright as children of God, which is expressed in the second line of the Mandate, to "be childlike."

On the other hand, if we have not been faithful to the Gospel, to living the Mandate, we shall not enter into God's rest, into the perfection that Jesus had called us to in the Gospel: "Be perfect as your heavenly Father is perfect":

> Therefore we must have before us the fear that while the promise of entering his rest remains open, one or another among you should be found to have missed his chance. For indeed we have heard the Good News, as they did. But in them the word they heard did them no good because they did not share the faith of those who listened.

> We, however, who have faith, shall reach this "rest," as in the text: "I vowed in my anger they shall never enter my rest." God's work was undoubtedly finished at the beginning of the world, as one text says referring to the seventh day: "After all his work, God rested on the seventh day."

> The text we are considering says, "They shall not enter my rest." It is established, then, that some people would reach this rest; and since those who first heard the Good News

failed to reach it through their disobedience, God fixed another day when, much later, he said, "Today" through David in the text already quoted: "Today if you hear his voice, do not harden your hearts.'

If Joshua had led them into this rest, God would not have spoken of another "day" after that. There must still be, therefore, a Sabbath Rest reserved for God's people; for anyone who enters rest, rests from his own work as God did from his. Let us then make every effort to enter that rest, so that no one may fall by following this evil example of disbelief (Heb 3:7-4, 11).

JESUS IS THE PROMISED LAND

This brings us, then, to the final meaning of the final word of the Mandate. We have said this "rest" refers to two realities in the Scripture: the Sabbath, understood as the perfection of a work, the integration of our lives; and secondly, the Promised Land.

Very simply, *Jesus himself is the Promised Land.* We are told to preach the Gospel, and the Gospel is God's love manifested in Jesus. *The awareness of Jesus as our Beloved is our "Rest."* He has said: "Come to Me all you who labor and are overburdened, and I will give you rest. Shoulder my yoke and learn from Me, for I am meek and humble of heart, and you shall find rest for your souls" (Mt 11:28, 29). Jesus himself is this rest. "His left arm is under my head and his right arm embraces me. I charge you, daughters of Jerusalem, not to stir my love, nor rouse her, until she pleases to awake" (Song of Songs, 8).

THE RESURRECTED CHRIST *AS OUR REST*

" CHRIST IS RISEN . . . VERILY HE IS RISEN . . . ALLELUIA! I think that is the essence of our apostolate, this resurrection of his. Let us remember that we are children of the resurrection." (SLFF 4, 1971)

I have quoted this text before, but let me repeat it here. In commenting on this last line of the Mandate, Catherine says: "Resting in the arms of God . . . we must walk in the heat of the day . . . go through everything he did. But we know something that nobody else knew in his day. *We know that we live in his resurrection.*" (COM)

"If you have risen with Christ, seek the things that are above" (Col 3:1). "We know that we have passed from death to life because we love the brethren" (1 Jn 3:14).

We believe that even now we live the life of the resurrected Christ himself. Because of our sins and our lack of purity of heart, we cannot experience the full splendor of this life. But he is in us: "I live now, not I, but Christ lives in me." We are still a mixture of the old and the new. But our life even now is essentially the same eternal life we shall live forever — now in a glass, darkly, then face to face. *To the extent that, by faith, we live in the reality of the resurrected Christ, to that extent we "rest" in this life.* The resurrected Christ will be our eternal life; he is even now our rest.

THE MUSIC OF EASTER

In the following passage we see how Catherine experienced all the great deeds of God in the light of the resurrection. The gloriously risen Christ was the Father's plan from all eternity, and everything must be seen in that light. The music of Easter surrounds all of reality:

Easter! A breathless feast of light and love! A Love
triumphant. Easter! A little word that holds the answer to
so many troubled hearts. . . .

The music of Easter is tremendous and yet, for those who
have ears to hear, it begins with the voice of the Almighty,
filled with accents of love, tenderness and compassion,
promising sinners — Adam and Eve — forgiveness, salva-
tion, and redemption. It continues through the mighty
voices of the prophets of old and comes to a climax in the
cry of a Child in a cave of Bethlehem — a Child who is also
God.

In that Easter music, the sounds of a small village in
Nazareth can be heard. The soft notes of wood shavings
falling on a floor. The daily, ordinary noises of living heard
from a street and that easily enter a carpenter's shop.

That music contains the voice of God speaking the words of
man as He walked with other men across the tiny land of
Palestine. The noises of that music hold within themselves
the almost unbearable symphony of his words at the last
Supper, words of Love, of Hope.

But they also hold the sound of whips, of a human hand
against a human cheek. Of the hundred voices of an angry
mob and of a moan, or was it the prayer, of Christ in
Gethsemane, and his last words on the Cross? And the
rending of a temple veil and of a strange, unearthly
earthquake.

The music that holds the silence of a tomb and the rolling
away of an immense stone. And, again, the voice of the
resurrected Christ speaking to many. And it holds the
sound that is almost soundless, and yet deafening, of the
victory of life over death and love over death.

Christ is risen! Let us now arise and go and preach his
Gospel with our lives. For it is because he is risen that we are
his. WE ARE CHRISTIANS! (R, April, 1966)

In the next passage Catherine speaks about "the little line of darkness." It is the line which results from our weak faith, our weak vision and experience of the depth of reality, which is the risen Christ:

> It began Good Friday. For already the cross and the tomb stood against the slowly reddening sky. Darkness is really evaporated.
>
> And Easter is light, so tremendously bright that you cannot even see the cross or the tomb or the people or anything around about. You can only see the light. This light penetrates every fiber of your being.
>
> Easter isn't over, you know. It's never over. It's always with us. Easter is a strange fabric. You turn it one way, and it's all light. You can see the light. You turn it a different way, and at the horizon there is a little line of darkness.
>
> Christ is in our midst. And where he is, there is the Father and the Spirit. All this is clearly understood. The tiny line should be accepted naturally, or shall we say, supernaturally, because constantly the light and the darkness mix to present to you his love.
>
> We can look at our lives this way and that, like we're examining a piece of cloth.. Now we see the resurrected Christ; now we see more the darkness of our old life. (Unpub. Talk, Easter, 1977)

I believe that, for Catherine, the "rest" of God is living in the resurrected Christ. This is the essence of the Apostolate, the essence of the Mandate, the essence of the Gospel. It is an ever-growing faith awareness that even now we are children of the resurrection. It is living in the consciousness of the ultimate victory of Christ within us.

As we grow towards love and poverty and all the other

dimensions of the Christ life, we grow also in living the resurrected life, because we are experiencing the triumph, in ourselves, of his Easter victory. "Rest," for Catherine, is living more and more *even now* in this eternal life that will never end.

As I bring this final volume of reflections on Catherine's Little Mandate to a close, I would now like to show *how she connects the Mandate with the resurrection and the resurrected Christ.* The Christ Catherine proclaims, the Christ she is in love with, the Christ who can transform the whole world, the Christ we are immersed in, is always the resurrected Christ, even though he mysteriously continues to suffer in his members. To live in the risen Christ is to be at rest. It is to have the apex of our spirit already living in the eternal life which shall never end.

PILGRIMAGING IN THE RESURRECTED CHRIST

I have never found this in Catherine's works, but we could understand the very first word of the Mandate — Arise! — as a call to live the new life of the resurrection. In Ephesians there is part of a very ancient Christian hymn: "Wake up from sleep, rise from the dead, and Christ will shine on you" (5, 14). The ancient Church called her children to throw off the slumber of the old life and be fully awake to the new dawn, the new life of Christ.

It is to be remembered, then, first of all, that the whole long journey of the pilgrimage to the lonely and risen Christ takes place *in the resurrection*:

> The pilgrim views everything he has and is as belonging to God and his brethren. His motto is "I am third: God,

neighbor, myself." Yes, that's the strange reality of a pilgrimage in the resurrected Christ.

The pilgrim in the resurrected Christ preaches the Gospel without ceasing, night and day. He isn't only preaching it, he is living it.

The reality of the pilgrimage in the resurrected Christ demands a surrender of one's will to God in a sort of totality. It demands that we do the most ordinary things — the duty of the moment — for it is the duty of God. And all the time we pilgrimage to attend to the duty of the moment. (St, 69-71)

Catherine here indicates that the whole Mandate is to be understood in terms of journeying *in the resurrected Christ*. And we so journey in the resurrected Christ because now *the whole world lives in the resurrected Christ*:

ALLELUIA! Christ is risen! Verily he is risen! Because he has risen, darkness has been conquered by light, death by life, hatred by love.

Now the world lives in the resurrected Christ. Whether men know it or not, the world has changed. It and the whole universe are now living, existing in the Lord of history, in the Lord of eternity, of time, and of love. Not only is the Church in pilgrimage toward the parousia, but so is man and all of his world, and everything that surrounds his world.

The resurrection of Christ brought love among us and is now the very principle of our existence. If only we recognize this we could transform the world. It's such a simple thing that only requires faith in the resurrected Christ!

Christians have received this gift of faith, and it should be the cradle of their love. For Love dwells in them and they in

Love. Love is God. It is so simple. Mankind needs love
more desperately than almost the air it breathes. Why not
start the fire of love by loving one by one all whom we meet
and deal with during the day. Then indeed the resurrection of Christ will become meaningful and our pilgrimage
to him will become joyful. (R, April, 1967)

The Mandate is a journey to the poor — "going to the
poor." It is the resurrected Christ who is present in the poor
of the world, which is everyone. In the following passage we
see that even though Christ still mysteriously suffers in his
members, it is always, as it was for Paul on the road to
Damascus — mystery of mysteries! — *the risen Christ who
needs to be consoled, the risen Christ who is present in suffering
humanity*:

Christ is risen! Yes, Lord, we see you clad in splendor.
Alleluia! But our hearts are heavy. All around us your
resurrected beauty suddenly changes into a million hungry
faces. The alleluias of our joy make jonquil carpets for your
pierced feet. But our hearts weep before the thousands
who are homeless — men, women, and children — the
victims of war and human greed.

Our eyes are dazzled by your resurrected glory. Yet, our
hearts behold the dark night of your loneliness in the
forsaken, the old, the forgotten.

Your resurrection has made the desert bloom. Yet, the
bitter smell of your poverty comes to us from the endless
lines of the pierced gray faces of the poor. They cry to us
who profess to follow you in many places.

Exultant is our soul with songs of gratitude and joy at the
conquest of death by you, O risen Lord. And yet, so many
of us will see your bloodstained face in the poor dead,
buried in some forgotten potter's field.

Christ is risen! Alleluia! Let us sing our alleluias, but let us also console him in all our brothers and sisters for whom he died, whoever they may be. Then indeed our alleluias will really mean what they were meant to mean: hope for new life for all men. (R, April, 1972)

We cannot believe in the resurrected Christ and fail to go out to the poor:

We cannot rejoice in the resurrection and be halfhearted Christians; it would be our condemnation. We cannot remain indifferent to the need of our brothers everywhere, for we are our brothers' keeper, because Christ came unto us, became man for us, and incarnated Himself for love of us. It is incredible that we can celebrate his resurrection in our churches with glad hearts, while our brothers across the world are denied their rights and privileges of human dignity and equality.

It is impossible that we can celebrate his resurrection in our churches while children, men, and women die from hunger in any corner of the world. Yes, the joyous, incredible feast of the resurrection of our Lord Jesus Christ must become a time for a deep, painful search of our consciences. This is the acceptable hour. (R, April, 1965)

Does the Gospel, the Mandate, seem impossible? Who can give up all you possess, preach the Gospel without compromise, go without fears into the depths of men's hearts? Is all this possible? Can the whole world become a community of love, a reflection of the Trinity? Is it an unreal dream?

No, it is not a dream. It is possible *because of the resurrection*:

Christ is risen! What does this message mean to the average
Christian in his ordinary daily life? It means hope. The
world belongs to those who give it hope. Christ gave it hope
— the supreme hope of love, of peace, of life everlasting.
Now it is the Christian's turn to continue to give that love
and that hope.

Because we have surrendered ourselves to Christ, because
we have accepted his Gospel in its totality, because we have
stripped ourselves of ourselves, he will be able to work his
healing process through us, and men will find that faith,
love and hope they so desperately seek. Then they too will
know that Christ is truly risen. Alleluia! (R, April, 1970)

Christ is risen! Now it is up to us to be witnesses to his
resurrection. To be a witness does not consist in engaging
in propaganda, nor even in stirring people up. It consists in
living a mystery — in being a living mystery. It means to
live in such a way *that people find hope in our presence, in the
presence of Christ in us.* (R, April, 1971)

We have been called to "preach the Gospel with our
lives." The Gospel that we have been called to preach is the
Good News of the resurrected Christ — God saying that he
still loves us even after we put his Son to death:

Easter, the greatest feast of the Christian world. . . . It
should awaken, arouse, draw, attract, compel, call, every
CatholicTO ARISE AND BECOME WHAT HE TRULY IS —
AN APOSTLE — ONE WHO IS SENT TO PREACH THE
GLAD TIDINGS OF THE RESURRECTION OF THE LORD
AFTER HIS INCARNATION, AND WHAT THAT RESUR-
RECTION MEANS TO US.

Which is but another way of arising and preaching the
Gospel of love to the marketplaces of the world, for the
glad tidings simply means THAT GOD LOVED US FIRST . . .

THAT OUR FAITH IS A LOVE AFFAIR BETWEEN GOD
AND US. AND THAT ALL WE HAVE TO DO, WE WHO
HAVE DIED AND RESURRECTED WITH HIM IN BAPTISM,
IS TO GO FORTH AND BY WORDS AND DEEDS TELL THE
WORLD ABOUT THIS INCREDIBLE GLAD NEWS THAT
GOD LOVES US!(R, March, 1964)

How like the first Easter this Easter of 1960 seems to be!
Now, as then, he appears to a small group before his
Ascension. For the number of the faithful . . . is both
expanding and shrinking. New worlds that lay dormant —
Africa and Asia — are arising. New giants. To these lands
modern apostles — priestly, religious and lay — will have to
go, even as the apostles had to go into unbelieving, pagan
worlds, to show them the living Christ, the Redeemer, the
Conqueror of Death, the Tremendous lover.

Alleluia! Alleluia! Christ is risen! Verily he is risen! Now, as
then, we must show him to our fellow countrymen in the
free world democracies that profess to believe in Him, and
yet, like Thomas, the apostle, are besieged by doubts and
temptations. And even as we sing, with heart, mind, and
soul, the joyous alleluias of Easter, let us all be sure that all
that Easter Sunday stands for, we bring to the marketplaces
of our disturbed and sorrowful world. (R, May, 1960)

We are called to love, to be a light to our neighbor's feet
in the midst of the darkness, to help establish communication in a world of isolation, to overcome our fears.

Withdrawal from other men leads us into hopelessness —
the narrow circle of living death, where all is silent and
where words are meaningless noises. We have gone
beyond the Tower of Babel days. We who *speak the same
tongue* have ceased to understand each other because our
words have become empty symbols of our own emptiness

and nothingness. How can we communicate with one another again? How can we restore ourselves to God and to each other? How can we implement the awesome reality of the mystery of the Mystical Body?

The answer is Easter, the feast of the resurrection. The feast of hope, the feast of love and of oneness. We, too, can resurrect ourselves from the tomb of silence and of withdrawal by faith and by love. We, too, can rise. We, too, can leave fears behind. For in him and in his resurrection we are all one. (R, April, 1962)

Finally, the resurrection is seen as the final goal.

Alleluia! We contemplate the apex of a fantastic mountain, the summit of the incomprehensible, the essence of all the joy of the world . . . THE RESURRECTION OF CHRIST. Each step up that mountain is a step into faith, the faith that is the true gift of God, and which he enlarges with every step of man.

Finally, as if having ascended a thousand Tabors, we behold Christ, risen from the dead!

But in our day so many stand at the foot of the mountain, looking upward, and say, "Where is the mountain?" They convince themselves that there was no resurrection. Others see the mountain, begin to climb it, but find it too hard; they descend back into the valley and remain there.

Then there are others who know that they cannot climb the mountain by themselves. They prostrate themselves at the foot of the mountain and cry out: "With your help alone shall we climb it. Hear us, Lord, extend your helping hand. We believe that Christ is the Messiah. We believe in his passion and resurrection. Help our unbelief."

All of us who live in the valley, all of us who must climb this
mountain of the Lord, must extend a hand to our brother
and say, "Let us climb together. In unity there is strength."
Then indeed will the valley be transformed, and everyone
will be climbing the mountain of the Lord, because
everyone will be helping each other to remember his face.

So let us all join hands and sing our alleluias in a loud voice.
Let it be a chorus of love to God, making us ready to follow
wherever the resurrected Christ leads us. (Unpub. Talk,
1988)

"The valley will be transformed." The valley is the human race, which could be transformed into the Body of the
risen Christ if everyone loved enough to take his brother
and sister by the hand and showed them the face of Christ.

THE PAROUSIA

In our "Way of Life" which Catherine wrote for our
community we read: "The Apostolate of Madonna House
and its members are pilgrims in this world proclaiming the
Second Coming of Christ, when all things will be restored in
him."

As is well known, "parousia" simply means "appearance." It is used by St. Paul referring to the final "appearing"
of the Lord Jesus Christ. This was a very rich and profound
reality for Catherine. We might even say that she lived not
only in the resurrected Christ but also in some profound
and mysterious way in the parousia. Each Sunday was not
only a little Easter but a little parousia as well. She lived in
the awareness that he could come again at any moment. She
lived in this heightened expectancy of his coming:

How clearly the Christians understood that each Sunday was a "little Easter" — that each was a parousia, for in each Christ came again in the mysteries and in the Eucharist. And, at the same time, each Sunday was the expectation of the parousia (the Second Coming of Christ). When this was to be, no one knew for sure, but all should be always expecting it!

That feeling, that flaming hope and expectation, was deeply rooted in the Russian heart, and it made all things bearable. All pains and sorrows were endurable, and it brought a mysterious understanding of the things that the human intellect alone cannot understand. It made the nights of life, with their stygian darkness, light with this hope.

It was an ever-present reality. It was spoken about amongst pilgrims and paupers. It gave buoyancy to all. It gave a zest for living, whilst, at the same time, taking away the fear of dying. FOR THERE WAS THE RESURRECTION AND THERE WAS THE PAROUSIA — HIS SECOND COMING. ALL WAS WELL, EVEN IF ALL SEEMED TO GO WRONG ON EARTH. (R April, 1961)

The Little Mandate is about life here on earth, so this is not the place to present Catherine's teaching about heaven. She never liked the idea of "eternal rest" as understood by most people! Just as the Little Flower, St. Therese, said she was going to spend her heaven doing good on earth, so I think this would more be Catherine's desire! Life for her was always movement and fire and vitality.

In one of the richest and most comprehensive of her expressions of the Mandate, she said: "For us to live in Nazareth we must, strange as it may seem, begin with Golgotha and the tomb! Then, resurrected in him, by his grace, we shall journey to Bethlehem with the knowledge of the resurrected Christ, and live in Nazareth in expectation of the parousia." (SL #183, 1965) It is by baptism that we are plunged into the tomb and then rise with Christ. Then we journey in life towards our original likeness as children of God, journey with the Holy Family in the spirit of Nazareth. And yes, we expect the *final* parousia, the *final* appearance of Christ. But Catherine once said this:

> Heaven is in persons — God, the saints, the saved ones. Heaven is in you, whatever it might be. And the "Credo" faith already brings you to the parousia. For the parousia is really the Trinity. The parousia is Our Lady. The parousia is all the saints and angels and everybody crying "Credo!" (Unpub. Talk, 1977)

> Easter! It holds within its alleluias and joy the promise of the Second Coming of the Lord, the parousia. That will truly bring us to the kingdom of God, and finally unite mankind once again to its Creator. (R, April, 1963)

In prayer, in the Eucharist, in her own interior journey, in others, Catherine not only met the lonely and risen Christ. She met "the Christ of the parousia," the Christ of the end time. This Christ of the parousia expresses an even deeper consummation, if we can put it that way, than the resurrected Christ. The resurrected Christ still suffers mysteriously in his Body, the Church. The Christ of the parousia is the Christ who, even now, sums up in himself the totality of the Father's plan. It is the "one Christ loving himself" of Augustine's final passage of the *City of God.*

It is this touching, in faith, of the Christ of the parousia which, I believe, constituted for Catherine the depths of resting: "Credo faith already brings you to the parousia." When your faith and life of love penetrates to this dimension of the Christ-life, then your human spirit is at rest. The promise, "I will be your rest" has been fulfilled and experienced as deeply as it can be in this life.

THE CHRIST OF THE EIGHTH DAY

In the Madonna House chapel in Combermere we have a magnificent icon entitled — "The Christ of the Eighth Day." "Parousia" means appearance. The Eighth Day, you might say, is one stage beyond the parousia! It is the EVERLASTING DAY that will never end, the final consummation of all Sabbaths, Sundays, Feast Days. To be immersed, by faith, in this "Christ of the Eighth Day," is to be at rest.

Thus, after the long journey to the lonely and in the risen Christ does the pilgrim arrive home in the Heart of the Trinity, and rest, through the power of the Holy Spirit, in Christ, the Eighth Day that has no end. It is to come home to the kingdom that has been prepared for those who met the lonely and risen Christ in the sick, the hungry, the naked, those in prison. Christ's Little Mandate to Catherine is a profound and trustworthy guide to all the pilgrims of the earth for making this journey. May it help to guide you, dear reader, along your pilgrimage. May your journey be filled with the music of Easter. And may we all meet on the Eighth Day and rejoice together forever!

I would like to give Catherine the last word. In her personal diary for May 22, 1954, she asks the Lord Jesus to grant her the very essence of his Little Mandate to her — to be always reposing on his Heart "while going about his business." It is a magnificent prayer for total union with the lonely and risen Christ until she sees him face to face. It can be our prayer to the lonely and risen Christ, asking his help to live the Mandate:

My days, my nights, minutes, seconds — are all his through Mary. That I know. But how is my heart? Does it rest in him always? Here I come before a baffling fact. I know one cannot "think" unceasingly of God, and yet, I also know that one can "rest in God" while going about his business.

O Lord of Peace, keep me within thy breast no matter where I am.

My feet may fly upon a thousand tasks for thee. My hands be busy with things to do for thee. My mind immersed in thoughts and deeds that all are there for thee.

But let my heart repose within thy heart. For then the rest of me will truly be blessed by thee.

I hunger so for that "repose" in thee. My heart is restless unless it rests in thee.

And as time goes by into the where time flies, my heart hungers more and more for silence and solitude.

I am so parched for both. It is like walking in a burning desert to be without them!

Oh grant me the grace of solitude amidst a milling throng! Of silence amidst all deafening noise! Of repose and rest within thy heart amidst activity on your behalf that never ceases.

O Lover, come and take possession of my heart — and keep it forever in your Sacred Heart.

KEY TO CITED WORKS

So as not to get too complicated, I have devised a simple key to the documents I am using. Sometimes I am working from the published editions; then I will quote the page reference. Sometimes I am working from original manuscripts; in that case I simply quote the work, since the public does not have access to the reference anyhow. I will list here also works of Catherine and others not used in this book so as to give the reader an overall view of her published works and other significant material.

AF - *Apostolic Farming.* Private printing.

CI - "The Church and I." Unpublished Talk.

COLM - "Comments on the Little Mandate." Unpublished Talk, 1969.

DB - *Dear Bishop* (New York: Sheed and Ward, 1947).

DBEL - *Dearly Beloved.* Three volumes. Catherine's staff letters to her community. We consider these the heart of her gospel formation of Madonna House. Madonna House Publications.

DF - *Dear Father* (New York: Alba House, 1978).

DLR - *Doubts, Loneliness, Rejection* (New York: Alba House, 1981).

DSem - *Dear Seminarian* (Milwaukee: Bruce Publishing Company, 1950).

FH - *Friendship House* (New York: Sheed and Ward, 1946).

FL - Furfey Letters. Catherine's correspondence with her former spiritual director, Fr. Paul Furfey, when she was in Harlem.

FML - *Fragments of My Life.* (Notre Dame, IN: Ave Maria Press, 1979).

GPW - *The Gospel of A Poor Woman* (Denville, NJ: Dimension Books, 1981).

GWC - *The Gospel Without Compromise* (Notre Dame, IN: Ave Maria Press, 1976).

HA - *The History of the Apostolate.* 3 Vols. Unpublished. Catherine's personal account of the history of her apostolate, starting in Toronto, then continuing in Harlem and Combermere.

HMCB - "How the Little Mandate Came To Be." Unpublished Talk, 1968.

ILI - *I Live On An Island* (Notre Dame, IN: Ave Maria Press, 1979).

JI & II - *Journey Inward.* Two volumes of Catherine's poetry privately published here at Madona House. I refer to it either as JI, I or JI, II. Some of these poems have been published. See next reference, *Lubov*, and *My Heart and I.*

JI - *Journey Inward* (New York: Alba House, 1984).

LDM - "Local Director's Meetings." Unpublished. These were talks given at our yearly meetings here at Madona House.

L - *Lubov* (Locust Valley, New York: Living Flame Press, 1985). Some of her poetry.

M - *Molchanie* (New York: Crossroad Publishing Co., 1982).

MHI - *My Heart and I* (Petersham, MA: St. Bede's Publications, 1987). Poetry.

MHWII - *Madonna House, What Is It?* Unpublished manuscript, 1980.

MRY - *My Russian Yesterdays* (Milwaukee: Bruce Publishing Company, 1951).

NWP - *Not Without Parables* (Notre Dame, IN: Ave Maria Press, 1977).

OC - *Out of the Crucible.* Some Ideas On Training For the Lay Apostolate. (New York: St. Paul's Publications, 1961).

OLUM - *Our Lady's Unknown Mysteries* (Denville, NJ: Dimension Books, 1979).

P - *Poustinia* (Notre Dame, IN: Ave Maria Press, 1975). Catherine's classic, now in over six languages.

Pov - *Poverty.* Unpublished manuscript. Catherine's final, comprhenseive statement on this aspect of the Gospel, 1980.

PTW - *The People of the Towel and the Water* (Denville, NJ: Dimension Books, 1978). Her best description of the Madonna House way of life.

R - *Restoration.* The monthly newspaper of Madonna House. (Only $4.00 a year!)

SC - *Stations of the Cross.* A Meditation. Private printing, 1954.

SL - *Staff Letters.* Unpublished letters of Catherine to her community of Madonna House.

SLFF - *Staff Letters from the Foundress.* A new series of the above, beginning in 1970.

SMHA - "The Spirit of the Madonna House Apostolate." A talk given in 1956.

SMS - *Soul of My Soul.* Reflections From a Life of Prayer (Notre Dame, IN: Ave Maria Press, 1985).

So - *Sobornost* (Notre Dame, IN: Ave Maria Press, 1977).

St - *Strannik* (Notre Dame, IN: Ave Maria Press, 1978).

TOLM - "Thoughts on the Little Mandate." Unpublished Talk given at the Directors' Meeting, 1969.

U - *Urodivoi*, Fools For God (New York: Crossroad Publishing Co., 1983).

WL - "Way of Life." The official Constitution of Madonna House written by Catherine, 1970-71.

WLIGI - *Where Love Is, God Is* (Milwaukee: Bruce Publishing Co., 1953).

OTHER WORKS

AIHLY - *As I Have Loved You.* (Dublin, Ireland: Veritas Publications, 1988). Omer Tanghe. An excellent popular presentation Of Madonna House by a priest who knows us well.

JLC - *Journey To The Lonely Christ.* The "'Little Mandate" of Catherine de Hueck Doherty (New York: Alba House, 1987). Robert Wild. This is the first volume of my trilogy on the mandate.

K - *Katia.* (Sherbrooke, Quebec: Editions Paulines, 1989).Emile Briere.

FLB - *For The Least Of My Brothers.* The Spirituality of Mother Teresa and Catherine Doherty. (New York: Alba House, 1989). Omer Tanghe. A series of letters to friends which shows the similarity between the spirituality of Mother Teresa and Catherine.

LLL - *Love, Love, Love.* (New York: Alba House, 1989). Robert Wild. This is the second of my volumes on the Little Mandate.

T - *Tumbleweed.* (Milwaukee: Bruce Publishing Company, 1948). Life of Catherine by her late husband, Eddie Doherty.